Federalism

ORIGIN, OPERATION, SIGNIFICANCE

BASIC STUDIES IN POLITICS

Under the Editorship of

SHELDON S. WOLIN

University of California, Berkeley

WILLIAM H. RIKER

Department of Political Science
University of Rochester

Federalism

ORIGIN
OPERATION
SIGNIFICANCE

LITTLE, BROWN
AND COMPANY
Boston and Toronto

LIBRARY OF CONGRESS CATALOG CARD NO. 64-22483

SECOND PRINTING

Published simultaneously in Canada
by Little, Brown & Company (Canada) Limited

PRINTED IN THE UNITED STATES OF AMERICA

Foreword

LIKE SO MANY areas of human knowledge today, the study of politics and political institutions is undergoing significant changes. A quarter-century ago only a few voices challenged the prevailing consensus regarding the methods of political science, the choice of problems, and the relative weight assigned to the "factors" shaping political events, actions, and behavior. Since then a revolution of uncertain proportions has occurred, one that has been variously described as "the behavioral movement" or "social science." It has visibly altered the climate of political science and it has deeply affected the outlook of the political scientist. No longer does he believe that political science is a self-contained field. It has become second nature for him to utilize methods, concepts, and data drawn from a wide range of academic disciplines, such as sociology, psychology, and economics.

A marked self-consciousness about methods of inquiry characterizes much of the contemporary literature, whereas thirty years ago only a few political scientists were troubled by this concern. Today's political scientist is receptive to quantitative techniques, eager to emphasize measurement, prepared to devise complex classifications of empirical data, ready to experiment with abstract models, and engrossed with the intricacies of preparing questionnaires and organizing surveys of public opinion. These changes in method have also affected the outlook and the language of political science. Where his predecessors talked of "comparative government," he is apt to talk of "comparative political systems"; where they referred to "the process of government," he prefers to examine "the theory of decision making"; and where they spoke simply of "political theory," he will, more often than not, insist on a distinction between "normative theory" and "empirical theory" and, depending on his candor or concerns, will assert that his main interest lies with the latter. It is perhaps inevitable that a moderate reaction should set in and that questions should be raised among political scientists about whether they have not gone too far and too fast. There is an uneasiness that some settled issues ought to be reopened; that important features of politics have been ignored; that questions of choice and value have to be restored to a central position; and that the wonder of politics has been lost amidst the preoccupation with abstractions, graphs, and mathematical tables.

In the light of these changes and uncertainties there is good reason for political scientists and political theorists to reflect on the changing nature of their field of study and to report to a less specialized, but no less interested, audience how political events, practices, and behavior appear to the contemporary political scientist; what way or ways of looking at these matters he has found most useful and fruitful; and what problems he considers to be genuine and important.

This series of books was designed for such a purpose. The authors do not attempt to provide simply a digest of relevant facts, but to offer reflections and systematic analyses of the more significant and interesting areas of political science and political theory. Some concentrate upon familiar topics, such as federalism and political parties, but they seek to suggest the theoretically interesting problems raised by these traditional themes. Other studies, such as those dealing with political theory and ideology, proceed on a more theoretical plane, but with the explicit intention of indicating their relevance to the empirical concerns of political science. The standard set for this volume by Professor Riker and for all the others is, I hope, within the best tradition of political science: the standard of reflective inquiry and informed analysis.

Federalism is a topic of peculiar interest to Americans. The greatest political classic of American political theory bears the title: *The Federalist*. The Constitution that settled our form of government was designed in the knowledge that this was to be the first self-conscious test of a federal system in the modern world. The constitution-makers of Philadelphia introduced an innovation in Western political theory and practice that, by its subsequent success, exercised considerable influence during the 19th and 20th centuries. No federal system, ancient or modern, has endured for so long. The American example has served as a point of departure for later experiments and today there are numerous examples of political systems, in the Western and non-Western worlds alike, which have been deliberately modelled upon the federal principle. Not all of these experiments have been successful. The most profound crisis in American history was, to a significant degree, a crisis in federalism. The *Sonderbundskrieg* in Switzerland was fought on the principle of secession and nearly destroyed the Swiss federation.

Although the problems connected with federalism have been of continuing concern to political scientists for more than a century, relatively few theoretical treatises of lasting significance have emerged. This failure of theory to keep pace with practice forms a curious historical parallel with the ancient world. The political genius of the Greeks also extended to the invention of several federal systems, but no philosopher appeared to grace that experience with the kind of immortality Plato and Aristotle had bestowed on the city-state. Perhaps the basic reason for that failure lay in the stubborn Greek conviction that the values of political life could only be enjoyed in the small setting of the *polis* and that a wider unity necessarily brought a dilution of political life. When we turn to consider the lack of American theorizing about federalism, we encounter the interesting fact that much of the literature has expressed the critical view that the federal system presents serious obstacles to the attainment of certain values by political means. Beginning with the agrarian revolts of the last quarter of the 19th century and extending down to the civil rights controversy of the present moment, many of the liberal movements of protest and reform have contended that a system that rested upon a distribution of authority between the central government and the states made it easy for parochial authorities and special interests to frustrate the majority's efforts to deal with such truly national problems as child labor, monopolistic practices in business, the wages, working conditions, and bargaining rights of labor, and racial segregation. Viewed in broad perspective, the literature of reform has been intent upon propounding a theory of anti-federalism that has seriously questioned the basic constitutional division of powers between nation and state. These attacks have been adequately challenged by the defenders of federalism, but it would be difficult to grant that they have done more than to rehearse the old arguments set forward in *The Federalist* and in the opinions of the "unreconstructed" Supreme Court.

One of the valuable aspects of the present study by Professor Riker is the demonstration that it is possible for a political scientist to combine a genuine theoretical outlook with an equally genuine concern for the crucial political issues currently agitating American society. The merit of the present volume rests on more than this one achievement. Someone has said that a good philosophy should be not only true but also interesting. Most discussions of federalism have satisfied the former criterion but rarely the latter. Anyone who has ever taught a college course about American government has experienced a growing sense of dismay when he has tried to excite undergraduate interest in the problems of federalism. Where he had found that a class would immediately respond to questions about the First Amendment, it would greet the Tenth Amendment with as much enthusiasm as it would a discussion of the homoöusian controversy of the 4th century.

What makes this study truly interesting is that it avoids the legal and administrative formalism that has been such a constant feature of most past studies, and that it also surveys federalism from a fresh point of view. The author has appropriated several of the recent advances in the theory of bargaining and has utilized them to fashion a novel theoretical approach to his subject. In this he has fulfilled one of the basic requirements of theorizing: he has stimulated the reader to look at the familiar in an unfamiliar way, to view the commonplace in an uncommon light. The theory that he advances is tested against American experience, and is applied as well to federal experiments in "mature" Western societies and to societies "in transition." Throughout the argument we are reminded that federalism represents a complex choice that may take many forms and may require many different conditions for its establishment and maintenance. Although the distinctive arrangements of federalism are singled out for attention, the author has made a serious effort to indicate the various ways in which the influence of federalism has affected the practices of the political parties, the actions or inactions of President and Congress, the process of legislation, and the American political culture as a whole. Finally, this study is sharply critical of federalism, particularly of its proven ability to frustrate the wishes of the majority. It may be that all readers will not agree with this conclusion, yet this is perhaps less important than the fact that in disagreeing they will have to contend against an argument that combines what is best in a political theory, theoretical rigor and civic concern.

Sheldon S. Wolin

UNIVERSITY OF CALIFORNIA, BERKELEY

For Kate and Mary

Preface

Years ago, when I first thought of writing something like this book, I wanted to make a truly comparative study of federalism, which seemed to me to be exactly the kind of subject about which we might easily utter testable generalizations. As a political scientist, I have always regretted that much of what passes as scientific investigation in our field is no more than elaboration of unique detail, *e.g.*, the case study of a particular event, the history of a particular institution, the evaluation of a particular policy, the description of a particular culture. Because of this excessive concern with the unique, it has seemed to me imperative for the development of political science that it be provided with testable and tested generalizations, even if their meaning is not the most exciting revelation about nature. The comparative study of federalism seems to me an excellent way to satisfy this imperative since (1) federalism is a precisely definable and easily recognizable constitutional artifact, (2) it has been used in enough instances to permit generalization but not in so many instances as to defy systematic examination, and (3) in all instances in the present world, the artifact of federalism is derived from one source (*i.e.*, the United States), but it is encased in diverse institutional and cultural settings so that one should be able to distinguish between general and local features of the artifact. Since, for these reasons, the subject seems likely to yield testable generalizations, I once planned to write a comparative study of federalism.

In time, however, I came to realize that this was far too pretentious a project for one man. Even though in the contemporary world all federalisms have one inspiration, the earlier world contained earlier kinds of federalism that both antedate and anticipate the invention of centralized federalism in Philadelphia in 1787. Furthermore, each instance of a federalism ancient or modern is imbedded in a set of unique local institutions, which themselves must be appreciated and understood. To acquire the information about history, the sensitivity to culture, and the linguistic competence to examine all these societies is more than any isolated scholar can do. So I revised my original project to something more manageable: a study of federalism as it appears in one society, with the object of generating hypotheses that can be tested against experience in other societies. Such a study might be described as semi-comparative and this is what is presented here. Most of the detail is about the United States, which is the only federal government I think I understand; but at least two questions generated out of detail about the United States are checked carefully against experience from either all or some other federalisms. Even though the analysis is only semi-comparative, however, it improves, so I believe, on most of what passes as the study of "comparative government" today in that it goes beyond mere description of foreign governments and actually attempts to assay some features of them.

Since this is, hopefully, a work in political *science*, the features of federalism I have tried to assay are rather different from those which are usually considered by constitutional historians and commentators on politics. Typically, federalism has been discussed as a moral evaluation: Is it good or bad? efficient or inefficient? For example, a recent essay on federalism in the *American Political Science Review* concerns whether or not state fiscal policies have conflicted with national policies in the United States. This concern is, of course, important only in connection with making good public policy. And these questions of public policy are interesting to the scientist as citizen, but not to the scientist as scientist. In this work, therefore, I have tried to relegate questions of morality and efficiency to the last and shortest chapter. Instead of the moral questions, I have tried to raise existential ones: What occasions the adoption of a federal government? What induces societies to keep federal governments they already have? For the former question I have demonstrated the existence of a necessary (but not sufficient) condition of adoption; and for the latter question I have indicated (but not demonstrated) a sufficient (but not necessary) condition of maintenance. In an absolute sense, this is a paltry achievement; yet in relation to the other achievements of political science, this demonstration and indication are a fairly considerable advance, which is why I take the trouble to offer them in this possibly too pretentious form.

I take the opportunity of this preface to thank Professors William T. Bluhm, Richard Fenno, Dale Neumann, and S. Peter Regenstreif, who read portions of the manuscript, and Mrs. Marguerite Gross, who typed several drafts.

William H. Riker

UNIVERSITY OF ROCHESTER

Table of contents

1

A THEORY OF FEDERALISM, 1

2

THE ORIGIN AND PURPOSES OF FEDERALISM, 11

3

THE MAINTENANCE OF FEDERALISM: THE ADMINISTRATIVE THEORY, 49

4

INSTITUTIONS OF FEDERALISM IN THE UNITED STATES, 85

5

FEDERALISM OUTSIDE THE UNITED STATES, 111

6

IS THE FEDERAL BARGAIN WORTH KEEPING? 137

SUGGESTIONS FOR FURTHER READING, 157

Federalism

ORIGIN, OPERATION, SIGNIFICANCE

I

A theory of federalism

This is an Age of Federalism. In 1964, well over half the land mass of the world was ruled by governments that with some justification, however slight, described themselves as federalisms. Thus,

in North America:	Canada, Mexico, and the United States
in South America:	Argentina, Brazil, and Venezuela
in Europe:	Austria, the Soviet Union, Switzerland, West Germany, and Yugoslavia
in South Asia:	Australia, India, Malaysia, and Pakistan
in Africa:	Congo, Ethiopia, and Nigeria

are all in one way or another federalisms. Furthermore, most of these governments are creations of the 19th and 20th centuries. The Swiss federation is of medieval origin; the United States was formed in the late 18th century; and the other federalisms in the Western Hemisphere were formed in the 19th century. Except for Germany, Austria, Switzerland, and Australia (which dates from 1901), the federalisms of the Eastern Hemisphere are products of the world-wide political reorganizations following the two world wars. Truly, the 20th century is an Age of Federalism, which is a constitutional bargain only rarely and sporadically struck prior to the 19th century.

I THE POPULARITY OF FEDERAL CONSTITUTIONS

The recent popularity of federal constitutions is not surprising because federalism is one way to solve the problem of enlarging governments — a problem that is one of the most pressing political concerns in the modern world. Like so many other modern problems, this one is a consequence of rapid technological change. Each advance in the technology of transportation makes it possible to rule a larger geographic area from one center, to fill a treasury more abundantly, to maintain a larger bureaucracy and police, and, most important of all, to assemble a larger army. There seem to be enough ambitious politicians in the world at any one time to guarantee that at least one government will use the new technology of transport to enlarge its area of control. And, once one government enlarges itself, then its neighbors and competitors feel compelled to do likewise in order, supposedly, to forestall anticipated aggression. Hence it is that technological change and a sense of competition together guarantee that governments will expand to the full extent that technology permits.

At the dawn of written history, most governmental units were tiny, consisting typically of an urban place and a few square miles of farms and villages. But with technological advance, imperial dominions became possible. Some of these in the ancient Near East and central and south Asia were based on the domestication of the horse; others like the Egyptian and Chinese were based on the exploitation of a river system as a channel of transport. The Roman empire is especially interesting for it was first created by control of the Mediterranean (*mare nostrum*) as a channel of transportation and was expanded by the invention of the Roman roads to control western Europe. Even so, the ancient empires were small by modern standards and at its height Rome probably ruled less land and fewer people than are now ruled from any one of these cities: Washington, Ottawa, Brazilia, Moscow, New

Delhi, Peking, and Canberra. A necessary condition for these numerous large governments of today is of course innovation in transportation. First came the navigational discoveries (compass, triangular sail, sextant, trigonometry, etc.) that permitted the so-called expansion of Europe and, second, the innovations in land transportation (the steam railroad, the automotive engine, road building and earth moving, the airplane, etc.).

The initial form of most of the great modern governments was empire. That is, large territories were accumulated by conquest when the technologically sophisticated Europeans subdued the relatively primitive inhabitants of America, Asia, and Africa. Thus were created the Spanish, Portuguese, Dutch, British, French, German, Russian, and Belgian empires. Of modern empires, only the Austrian, Turkish, and Chinese involved the conquest of territory inhabited by people as technologically sophisticated as the conqueror and even in these cases the conqueror had some kind of technological superiority in transportation and military equipment.

But empire, which was the characteristic form of European domination of the world in the 18th and 19th centuries, has not been popular or successful in the 20th. I think there are at least two reasons for the contemporary failure of imperialism. One is that the imperial powers exhausted themselves in conflict with each other so that they were no longer strong enough to control their dependencies. This is a process that started as early as the several American revolutions against England, Spain, and Portugal, all three of which were weakened or diverted by intra-European warfare at the time the revolutions occurred. Today this process is ending as Africans gain freedom from the European empires debilitated by two world wars. A special case, but still a part of this process, is the dismemberment of a defeated empire after an inter-imperial war, as when the German and Turkish empires were divided up by the winners in 1919 or when the United States took over the remnants of the Spanish empire in 1898. The other reason for the failure of imperialism is that the dependencies learned enough modern technology from their masters to challenge imperial control. (Those dependencies largely inhabited by descendants of European emigrants were, of course, the quickest to learn and the first to challenge, as in North and South America; but by the 20th century even most of the indigenous peoples had learned enough to rebel.) For these two reasons, therefore, the imperial form of territorial expansion has gradually been discarded — and as the discarding goes on, the very act of discarding itself contributes to further discarding, as exemplified by the recent and continuing dismemberment of the Dutch, Belgian, and Portuguese empires, all of which have been ludicrous anachronisms in the 20th century and all of which are now collapsing almost in sympathetic imitation of the collapse of the British and French empires.

The collapse of imperialism forces a constitutional alternative on all successful rebels: Since they necessarily rebel within the subdivisions established by the imperial power for its own convenience in governing, one alternative is to establish the freed subdivisions as independent political units. But the subdivisions, coordinated as they have been by the colonial office in the center, are not usually large enough to take advantage of the technological conditions that made the empire possible in the first place. Hence, if the newly independent subdivisions stand alone as political entities, they are highly vulnerable to yet a new imperialism. This is what happened, for example, to the Balkan rebels against the Austrian and Turkish empires. Freed from one imperial master as a result of 19th-century revolutions and World War I, and yet too small to support large armies, they fell victim in World War II to Hitler's abortive Third Reich and then to Stalin's Communist hegemony. The whole of Africa and the Near East is now Balkanized in a similar way and it is not fanciful to suggest that something of a similar future awaits these new nations. The other alternative for successful rebels is to join several former imperial subdivisions together. But if they join the subdivisions in one centralized political unit, then the rebels have merely exchanged one imperial master for a lesser one. Thereby much of the justification for rebellion is lost. The subdivisions can, however, be joined in some kind of federation, which preserves at least the semblance of political self-control for the former subdivisions and at the same time allows them (by means of the government of the federation) to make use of the technological advantages in the size of treasuries and armies and thus to compete successfully with their neighbors.

In this sense federalism is the main alternative to empire as a technique of aggregating large areas under one government. Although it probably does not so clearly assure large treasuries and armies, it does assure them to some degree — and it avoids the offensiveness of imperial control. It is this combination of attributes, I believe, that accounts for the 20th-century popularity of the federal kind of constitutional bargain and explains why today all the governments of large territories (except China) have federal constitutions at least in name.

II KINDS OF FEDERAL CONSTITUTIONS

Only in the modern world, however, has federalism been an effective alternative to empire. Although the notion of federalism has existed from ancient times, ancient and medieval federalisms (with one exception) succumbed rather quickly to imperial onslaught. By contrast, modern federalism has been notably successful, at least in the Western Hemisphere. Much of the reason for this difference in performance stems from the invention in 1787 of a new kind of federalism, so that in the modern world *centralized* federalism has generally replaced the *peripheralized* federalism characteristic of earlier eras.

The essential institutions of federalism are, of course, a government of the federation and a set of governments of the member units, in which both kinds of governments rule over the same territory and people and each kind has the authority to make some decisions independently of the other. But this notion admits of a great many actual constitutional arrangements, some of which may operate effectively and others may not. The numerous possible federal constitutions may be arranged in a continuum according to the degree of independence one kind of the pair of governments has from the other kind. The range of possibilities in this relationship is between the following minimum and maximum:

minimum: the ruler(s) of the federation can make decisions in only one narrowly restricted category of action without obtaining the approval of the rulers of the constituent units. (The minimum is *one* category of action, not zero, because if the ruler(s) of the federation rule nothing, neither a federation nor even a government can be said to exist.) Some ancient federations were federations in this minimal sense because their rulers were authorized to make decisions independently only about military tactics and then only during the course of a battle.

maximum: the ruler(s) of the federation can make decisions without consulting the rulers of the member governments in all but one narrowly restricted category of action. (The maximum number of categories is *all but one*, not simply all, because, if the rulers of the federation rule everything, the government is an empire in the sense that the rulers of the constituent governments have *no* political self-control.) The Soviet Union may be an example of a federation at the maximum. Although the government of this federation is, by its written constitution, one of delegated powers somewhat like that of the United States, still the guarantee of independence to constituent units seems only nominal, except, perhaps, in the area of providing for the cultural life of linguistic and ethnic minorities around whom the union republics are constructed. If, in fact, the union republics are fully able to decide about cultural life without consultation with the government of the federation, then the Soviet Union is a totally centralized federalism. If, however, the union republics cannot freely decide even in this area, then the Soviet Union is an empire, not particularly different from the Tsarist empire it succeeds.

Of course, relatively few federalisms lie at either extreme. Those which lie in between are spaced according to the number and importance of the areas of action in which the ruler(s) of the federation decide(s) independently of the rulers of the subordinate governments. Those which are closer to the maximum than to the minimum are described as *centralized*, whereas those closer to the minimum than to the maximum are *peripheralized*.

Although this distinction between kinds of federalisms seems fairly precise, the precision is somewhat spurious. There is no mechanical means of totting up the numbers and importance of areas of action in which either kind of government is independent of the other. Both the notion of number of categories and the notion of importance are evaluative and hence relative to the cultures from which each specific federalism springs. Nevertheless, there is one rough standard by which it is possible to assign any particular federalism to one category or the other. If a federalism is centralized, then the ruler(s) of the federation have and are understood to have greater influence over what happens in the society as a whole than do all the rulers of the subordinate governments. And, having this influence, they tend to acquire more. Thus, an identifying feature of centralized federalism is the tendency, as time passes, for the rulers of the federation to overawe the rulers of the constituent governments. Conversely, if a federalism is initially peripheralized, the rulers of the subordinate governments have, in sum, greater influence over the affairs of the whole society than do the ruler(s) of the federation. Having the initial advantage, the rulers of the subordinate governments tend to acquire more; and thus an identifying feature of peripheralized federalism is the tendency, eventually, for the rulers of the constituent governments to overawe the ruler(s) of the federation. Using these standards, observation of the historical development of particular federalisms enables the observer to assign them to either the centralized or the peripheralized category.

Once these standards for categorization have been enunciated, the significance of the distinction between centralized and peripheralized becomes apparent. Peripheralized federalisms — with their tendency to minimize the role of rulers of the federation, with their tendency to permit the rulers of the constituent units to aggrandize themselves at the expense of the federal officials, and with their tendency to allow even those decisions originally intended for the rulers of the federation to revert to the rulers of the subordinate governments — can hardly be expected to provide effective government. They fall gradually apart until they are easy prey for their enemies. Centralized federalisms, on the other hand, become more like unitary or imperial governments in time and thus render the whole federation able to function more effectively in a hostile world. It is this difference between gradual disintegration and gradual solidification that explains the contrast between the failure and relative rarity of ancient and medieval peripheralized federalisms and the success and popularity of modern centralized ones.

III ANCIENT AND MEDIEVAL PERIPHERALIZED FEDERALISMS

The first appearance of what can be called federal governments occurred in ancient Greece after the Peloponnesian War. The circumstances that inspired the invention were exclusively military, either the threat of Sparta, the threat of Macedon, or the threat of Rome, all three of which were imperial powers that promised to and in fact did absorb the miniscule city-states that tried to defend themselves with a federal combination. Since the exclusive purpose of these federations was military, the constituent cities delegated to the federal rulers only military authority, retaining for themselves decisions on diplomatic matters such as whether or not to make war, whether or not to conclude treaties, and other affairs highly relevant to military decisions. As a consequence, the military function was ill-performed; the poor performance was used by the rulers of constituent units as a justification for further restrictions on the authority of the federal military officials; and such restriction led in turn to even worse military performance. First Macedon, then Rome, triumphed. And the notion of federalism was not heard of again until the Middle Ages.

It reappeared when circumstances essentially similar to those of the Greek city-states were replicated. In northern Italy and southern Germany medieval cities formed military federations to resist the encroachments of nascent nation states, all of which were essentially imperial in nature. These Italian and Suabian federalisms went through exactly the same cycle as the Greek federalisms had 1,500 years earlier and for exactly the same reasons. Only one of them survived into the modern world: the Swiss confederation — and it survived not because of its constitutional form but because of its unique geographic advantages for defensive military operations.

In the 16th century the Dutch federation was formed as an incident in the struggle for the independence of the low-country bourgeoisie from the feudal imperialism of the Spanish crown. This federation survived for over 200 years (until formally demolished by Napoleon), although it was for all practical purposes a simple monarchy after 1672. Nevertheless the Dutch federation represented a major constitutional innovation as compared with earlier federalisms, for, though legally peripheralized, it was considerably more centralized than any had previously been. Most of the time it consisted of seven provinces, of which by far the richest, strongest, and most populous was Holland with its cities of Amsterdam and Rotterdam. Legally, the authority to make all important diplomatic and military decisions was vested in the rulers of the provinces, but in fact these decisions were transferred either to stadtholders or other federal officials. The stadtholders were princes, William the Silent and his heirs. They were elected by provincial officials; but when the line of Orange was ascendant most of the provinces elected the same man. Thus the military and diplomatic unity of the Netherlands as a whole rested in the joint selection of this one federal official. Indeed, when a stadtholder existed, the Dutch federation was probably centralized into a monarchy. When a stadtholder was not chosen, however, decisions for the federation were made by a central parliament, which was legally subject to control on all important issues by the provincial parliaments. This highly peripheralized constitution was circumvented, however, by two institutional arrangements: First, the representatives of Holland usually were able to control the whole parliament by either bribery or force; and second, the most important governmental functions were performed by a board of admiralty which was so constructed as to give effective control to the merchants of Amsterdam and which governed both the navy (the main military force) and overseas trading companies (the main commercial concentration). In either case the oligarchy of Amsterdam controlled the whole federation in a quasi-imperial manner. In short, the Dutch republic, though legally a peripheralized federalism, succeeded and survived because beneath the peripheralized legal forms it provided for centralization either under a stadtholder or under the

Amsterdam merchants. When it conformed somewhat to its legal structure it suffered military and diplomatic reverses. When it deviated extra-legally from its constitutional forms, it was a great European power until eclipsed by the even more formidable imperial centralization of Napoleonic France.

IV MODERN CENTRALIZED FEDERALISMS

Although the Dutch federalism was only extra-legally centralized, the American federalism after 1787 was legally and constitutionally centralized. The innovation involved in this new government is the crucial event in the history of federalism and for that reason it will be examined in detail in the next chapter. It is sufficient to say now that the first American federalism (established informally in 1776 and formally in 1781) was modelled on the ancient federalism and on the supposed structure of the Dutch republic. So long as the Revolutionary War was in progress and all the really important federal decisions rested in the hands of the military commander, General Washington, the peripheralized feature of the government under the Articles of Confederation did not impede effective action by the central government. As soon as the war was over, however, this peripheralized federalism began, characteristically, to fall apart. The reform of 1787 transformed the federation into a centralized one, which survived and prospered. Because it prospered, other constitution-makers copied it. These adaptions also prospered and were copied, until now, as I previously noted, over half the world is ruled by federal governments.

Thus the scene is set for the contemporary popularity of federalism. In the next chapter, the spread of the federal idea will be examined in detail by analysis of the main features of the origin of all federalisms that have existed since 1787. Though analytically arranged, this summary can also serve as an historical introduction to the development of the federal bargain into a variety of forms.

2

The origin and purposes of federalism

IN THE previous chapter I interpreted federalism as a bargain between prospective national leaders and officials of constituent governments for the purpose of aggregating territory, the better to lay taxes and raise armies. This bargain can be defined quite precisely so that, when presented with an instance of a constitution, one can say whether or not it belongs to the class of federalisms. The rule for identification is: A constitution is federal if (1) two levels of government rule the same land and people, (2) each level has at least one area of action in which it is autonomous, and (3) there is some guarantee (even though merely a statement in the constitution) of the autonomy of each government in its own sphere. Since such constitutions have appeared frequently in the last century and three-quarters, the class of federal bargains is large enough to admit of some generalizations involving it. Because the class is both precisely defined and relatively large, one can rise above the undisciplined uniqueness characteristic of historical commentary, even though each instance of a federal bargain is of course imbedded in a unique historical context.

I CONDITIONS OF THE FEDERAL BARGAIN

As bargains, the acts of making federal constitutions should display the main feature of bargains generally, which is that all parties are willing to make them. Assuming that they do display this feature, one may ask what it is that predisposes the parties to favor this kind of bargain. From the theory set forth in the previous chapter, I infer the existence of at least two circumstances encouraging a willingness to strike the bargain of federalism:

1. The politicians who offer the bargain desire to expand their territorial control, usually either to meet an external military or diplomatic threat or to prepare for military or diplomatic aggression and aggrandizement. But, though they desire to expand, they are not able to do so by conquest, because of either military incapacity or ideological distaste. Hence, if they are to satisfy the desire to expand, they must offer concessions to the rulers of constituent units, which is the essence of the federal bargain. The predisposition for those who offer the bargain is, then, that federalism is the only feasible means to accomplish a desired expansion without the use of force.
2. The politicians who accept the bargain, giving up some independence for the sake of union, are willing to do so because of some external military–diplomatic threat or opportunity. Either they desire protection from an external threat or they desire to participate in the potential aggression of the federation. And furthermore the desire for either protection or participation outweighs any desire they may have for independence. The predisposition is the cognizance of the pressing need for the military strength or diplomatic maneuverability that comes with a larger and presumably stronger government. (It is not, of course, necessary that their assessment of the military–diplomatic circumstances be objectively correct.)

For convenience of abbreviation I shall refer to these two predispositions as (1) the expansion condition and (2) the military condition.

The hypothesis of this chapter is that these two predispositions are *always* present in the federal bargain and that each one is a necessary condition for the creation of a federalism. I am tempted, on the basis of my immersion in this subject, to assert that these two conditions are together sufficient. But, since I cannot possibly collect enough information to prove sufficiency, I am constrained to assert only the more modest hypothesis of necessity.

In order to prove this hypothesis, I have examined *all* the instances of the creation of a federalism since 1786, giving most detailed attention to the invention of centralized federalism in the United States. (More exactly, I have examined all the instances I have been able to discover. It is quite possible, however, that I have overlooked some obscure instances.) For those federalisms which have survived, I am able to show that the two conditions existed at the origin; and, for those which failed, I am able to show that either the conditions never existed or they existed only momentarily. Though such evidence does not constitute absolute proof of the hypothesis, it comes as close to a proof as a non-experimental science can offer.

Before this proof is undertaken, a word about the significance of this hypothesis. To those whose first acquaintance with the literature on federalism was the introductory chapter of this book, the hypothesis may seem obvious and trivial. But it is not; and to show why it is not I shall briefly examine two widely asserted fallacies about the origin of federalism.

One is the ideological fallacy, which is the assertion that federal forms are adopted as a device to guarantee freedom. Numerous writers on federalism, so many that it would be invidious to pick out an example, have committed this ideological fallacy. It is true, of course, that federalism does involve a guarantee of provincial autonomy and it is easy to see how some writers have confused this guarantee with the notion of a free society. Indeed, in certain circumstances, for example by encouraging provinces to have different policies or even simply to be inefficient, federalism may provide interstices in the social order in which personal liberties can thrive. And I suppose it is the observation of this fact that leads one to the ideological fallacy.

The worst error involved in this fallacy is the simple association of (1) federalism and (2) freedom or a non-dictatorial regime. Only the most casual observation of, for example, the Soviet Union or Mexico demonstrates, however, that even though all the forms of federalism are fairly scrupulously maintained, it is possible to convert the government into a dictatorship. In the two examples mentioned, the conversion has been accomplished by a strict one-party system, which suggests that the crucial feature of freedom is not a particular constitutional form, but rather a system of more than one party. (See Chapter 5, *infra.*) But in other countries, *e.g.*, Brazil, Argentine, imperial Germany, even federalism and a multi-party system have been unable to prevent dictatorships, so probably some even more subtle condition is necessary to maintain free government. What it is I cannot say, but I am certain that there is no simple causal relationship between federalism and freedom.

Even though it is objectively false that federalism preserves freedom, it is still possible that uninformed constitution-writers might believe they were providing for freedom simply by making the federal bargain. And if they did, then the ideological fallacy would be no fallacy at all. But there is almost no evidence that they have so believed, or at least no evidence that such a belief was a primary motivation. Theoretically, it is unlikely that writers of federal constitutions are so motivated. As men engaged in expanding a government, they are much more likely to be preoccupied with practical expedients for the moment than with provisions for the distant and not clearly foreseen future. As centralizers, they are much more likely to be concerned with centralization itself than with fears that centralization may go too far. Entirely apart from these theoretical considerations, however, there simply is almost no evidence that they have been motivated in the way the ideological fallacy asserts. Most so-called evidence for this proposition is essentially anachronistic in nature, *e.g.*, citations from *The Federalist* papers to indicate the motives of the framers six months previously, conveniently overlooking that the authors of *The Federalist* papers throughout the

Convention were in favor of unitary government and had almost nothing to do with the invention of centralized federalism. If one examines the debates of authors of federal constitutions and the political circumstances surrounding them, as is done in the rest of this chapter, it is abundantly clear that practical considerations of expansion rather than ideological considerations of safeguards for freedom animated framers of federalisms. Only in the instances of Latin American federalisms can even moderately convincing cases be made for the latter motivation and under close examination, as I will show, even these instances collapse.

Alongside the rather crude ideological fallacy is the subtler and initially more impressive reductionist fallacy, which is the assertion that federalism is a response to certain social conditions that create some sense of a common interest. On the basis of a theory of this sort, British colonial administrators have encouraged a number of federalisms, some successful, some not. It is the fact of some failures that is interesting—for they indicate the inadequacy of the theory. Perhaps the most exhaustive statement of this kind of theory is contained in the work of Deutsch and his collaborators,[1] who produced a list of nine "essential conditions for an amalgamated security-community" of which class the class of federalisms is a sub-class:

> (1) mutual compatibility of main values; (2) a distinctive way of life; (3) expectations of stronger economic ties or gains; (4) marked increase in political and administrative capabilities of at least some participating units; (5) superior economic growth on the part of at least some participating units; (6) unbroken links of social communication, both geographically between territories and sociologically between different social strata; (7) a broadening of the political elite; (8) mobility of persons at least among the politically relevant strata; and (9) a multiplicity of ranges of communications and transactions.

There are many defects in such a list. It is apparent that these conditions are not sufficient to bring about amalgamation for, if they were, federalisms like the Central American Federation would never have broken up or a pan-Arabic movement would

[1] Karl Deutsch, *et al.*, *Political Community in the North Atlantic Area* (Princeton: Princeton University Press, 1957) p. 58.

reunite the Arabic parts of the former Turkish empire. Nor are all these conditions necessary, for a great many successful amalgamations have violated some or even all of them, *e.g.*, the Swiss confederation seems to have violated conditions (1) and (2) during most of its history and 19th-century colonial empires violated almost all conditions. If these conditions are neither jointly necessary nor sufficient, it is hard to imagine in what sense they are "essential."

The trouble with the Deutsch list is that it attempts to reduce the explanation of the political phenomenon of joining together to an explanation of the social and economic condition of the population. In bypassing the political, in bypassing the act of bargaining itself, it leaves out the crucial condition of the predisposition to make the bargain. What this list amounts to is a set of frequently observed conditions in which politicians can develop a predisposition to unite in some way or another. But it omits any mention of the political conditions in which, given some of these and other social and economic conditions, the actual predisposition to bargain occurs. The theory I have set forth, on the other hand, is confined to the political level entirely. It assumes some sense of common interest, of course, and then asserts the invariant conditions of forming one kind of larger political association, namely, federalism. (Incidentally, by confining the theory to a specific kind of amalgamation, the theory has a political focus that Deutsch and his collaborators failed to achieve.)

II THE INVENTION OF CENTRALIZED FEDERALISM

American historians have long disputed about the reason for the replacement of the peripheralized federalism of the Articles of Confederation by the centralized federalism of the Constitution. The traditional and long-prevailing explanation, which reached its most complete formulation in the writings of John Fiske (ca. 1890), was the teleological assertion that a more centralized union than the Articles could provide was needed for the United States to fulfill its destiny. This notion, however flattering to American readers, was, of course, chronological nonsense since the politicians of the 1780's could have at best a dim view of the "destiny" of the United States of 1890 or 1960.

As against this mystical explanation, Charles Beard in 1913 offered a wholly naturalistic explanation that, however, so denigrated heroes and assumed so naive a theory of social causation that it continued to be a center of controversy for nearly 50 years. Beard called his explanation an *economic* interpretation, by which he meant that the motive of those who wrote and supported the Constitution as against the Articles was simply the desire to get rich or stay rich. Assuming that the central feature of politics was the struggle between the haves and the have-nots, Beard argued that the have-nots preferred the peripheralized federalism of the Articles to the centralized Constitution proposed by the haves. In some places he even goes so far as to argue that the evil rich succeeded in imposing their Constitution on the meek poor only by chicanery. Naturally, this oversimplified attribution of motives and morals is easy to challenge and in the last decade the so-called revisionist historians have in fact shown, *inter alia*, that in some states it was the rich who opposed and the poor who favored the Constitution.[2]

Mere revision of Beard's historical errors is not likely, however, to improve our understanding of the constitutional change. What is needed is a broader conception of the nature of politics than Beard's narrow progressivism. In the following paragraphs, therefore, I have outlined what I call the "Military Interpretation of the Constitution of the United States" and have demonstrated that it accounts for the total local, national, and international features of the process of constitution-writing.

The Military Interpretation of the Constitution. From the end of the War of 1812 until the manufacture of an atomic bomb by the Soviet Union, most Americans felt safe from European invasion. During that long period (in the latter part of which Beard wrote), it was difficult to conceive of the international situation of the American states in the 1780's, when European aggression seemed both imminent and inevitable. (Probably this continental security that permitted exclusive preoccupation with domestic affairs was

[2] Charles Beard, *An Economic Interpretation of the Constitution of the United States* (New York: Macmillan, 1913); Robert E. Brown, *Charles Beard and the Constitution* (Princeton: Princeton University Press, 1956).

a precondition of Beard's misinterpretation of history.) But in the 1950's and 1960's it is again easy to sympathize with the fears and calculations of politicians of the era of the Articles. Consider the objective international situation they found themselves in. The thirteen states concluded in 1783 a very uneasy peace with the imperial power, uneasy because significant politicians in Britain regretted the outcome and hoped to reopen the war, and uneasy because it appeared likely that some of the states would give them occasion to do so. The British occupied forts in the Northwest Territory, forts which they were obligated to surrender under the terms of the Treaty of Paris but which they refused to surrender until the states paid the arrears in the treaty-obligated indemnity for Tory property seized during the war. The English threat in the Northwest was matched by the Spanish threat in the Southwest, where New Orleans was a base for potential expansion into the Ohio and Tennessee valleys. The States had neither fleet to forestall invasion nor army to repel it. In such circumstances wise politicians could seldom be free of the fear of war and in fact they were not. The chief criticisms they made of the peripheralized federalism of the Articles was that the system as a whole, central and constituent governments together, was inadequate for war and the prospect of war. I cite three instances: (1) Washington in his semi-annual political surveys to Lafayette throughout 1785 to 1787 emphasized the military weakness of government under the Articles. He seemed especially disturbed by the possibility that Kentucky might even voluntarily go with Spain. The military emphasis of these summaries, which presumably give Washington's considered judgment of the total political situation, probably explains why he attended the Philadelphia convention and by his sanction gave it a chance of success; (2) Madison, who is often called the father of the Constitution in the sense that he came to Philadelphia with a considered plan of reform and succeeded, of course, with Washington's approval, in writing the substance of it into the Constitution, circulated in 1786 a manuscript criticism of the Articles. The first, the longest, and the most passionately argued items in the list of weaknesses of the Articles all refer to the military or diplomatic inadequacies of Congress. Indeed, five items out of eleven are on this subject. Because Madison subsequently wrote the tenth *Federalist* paper, with its interpretation of domestic conflict in economic terms, Beard and his followers have supposed that Madison, like them, saw the great issue of the times as a domestic conflict among a variety of economic interests. But Madison's own writings on the Articles say otherwise and, as I shall show in item (3), only a wilful misinterpretation of *The Federalist* can align Madison with Beard.[3] (3) *The Federalist* papers, the main propaganda document issued in support of the ratification of the Constitution, emphasizes the military–diplomatic advantages of centralized federalism. *The Federalist* has, I recognize, been used to prove many and contradictory propositions about the Constitution. Nevertheless I point out that the first five papers — and presumably the first papers were regarded by its authors as of primary importance — are concerned with military and foreign affairs and were written by John Jay, who was then regarded as the great specialist on diplomacy. The structure of *The Federalist* and the content of its first papers thus suggests the primacy of military considerations in the process of centralization, at least in the understanding of the authors of that work.

These three instances, chosen from the main writers and writings responsible for the Constitution, do strongly suggest the primacy of the military motive in the adoption of centralized federalism. The suggestion is in fact so strong that one wonders how Beard and his followers could ever have believed that the main issues at Philadelphia were domestic matters of the distribution of income. The conflict between the military and economic interpretations is over what was the "main" issue. Naturally, the fathers of the Constitution were interested in both international and domestic affairs and when they talked about a better army sometimes they referred to the international scene and sometimes to the maintenance of order at home (especially to the policing of revolts by poor farmers, such as Shays' rebellion). Unques-

[3] See for example J. Fitzpatrick, *Writings of George Washington* (Washington, D.C.: Government Printing Office) Vol. 29, pp. 260-261 (15 Aug. 1787, to Lafayette); G. Hunt, *Writings of James Madison* (New York: G. P. Putnam and Sons, 9 vols., 1900-1910) Vol. 2, pp. 361-369, "Vices of the Political System of the United States."

tionably the Beardians were right when they said that some economic concerns were felt, but they were perversely wrong when they magnified the domestic concerns and ignored the foreign concerns almost entirely. Probably they did so because in their day foreign concerns were not very important anyway; but as I have shown, the preconceptions of their era were such that they could not easily sympathize with politicians who daily expected to be involved in European wars on the American continent. This is why they have distorted the message and the structure of *The Federalist*, why they have written incessantly of Shays' rebellion (which did indeed disturb Washington), but totally ignored Washington's much greater fear that the Kentuckians might join Spain, why they have emphasized the writings and views of provincial and insignificant leaders like Luther Martin, George Mason, *et. al.*, and largely ignored the writings of a really national and significant leader like Washington. It is almost as if some future historians of India were to interpret the history of constitution-making in that country with the words of Ambedekar and Narayan without discussing the words of Gandhi and Nehru.

The Bargain at Philadelphia. Taking it as proved that the fathers of the Constitution were primarily concerned with rendering their federalism better able to meet military and diplomatic threats, we may ask now how they proposed to improve its capabilities. This question leads us directly into the nature both of centralized federalism and of the bargain invented at Philadelphia in 1787.

The Virginia delegation at Philadelphia came prepared with a plan for a new constitution (presumably written by Madison and endorsed by Washington) which was essentially unitary in character. It provided that the people at large would elect the lower house of the national legislature and that this body in turn would choose all the remaining parts of a national government: an upper house, an executive, and a judiciary. Furthermore, it proposed to give an essentially unlimited grant of power to the national legislature

> to legislate in all cases to which the separate States are incompetent, or in which the harmony of the United States may be in-

> terrupted by the exercise of individual Legislation; to negative all laws passed by the several States, contravening in the opinion of the National Legislature the articles of Union; and to call forth the force of the Union agst any member of the Union failing to fulfill its duty under the articles thereof.[4]

This arrangement seems to be an adaptation of the unitary English constitution to fit a society lacking a formal aristocracy and royalty. Had the Virginia Plan been adopted and successfully imposed, federalism in North America would have ceased to exist. But the Virginia Plan was far too extreme a change to win acceptance in the Convention and so it was repeatedly modified. The invention of centralized federalism was thus a byproduct of modifications made to render the plan acceptable to ruling factions in the states. One cannot say that the framers tried to invent what they did — rather they tried to construct, by means of *ad hoc* arrangements, a government that would work in their own peculiar circumstances. By happenstance it embodied a principle that could also work in numerous other circumstances.[5]

The general theme of the modifications in the Virginia Plan was, as I have just indicated, to deviate from the unitary form just enough to render the plan acceptable to ruling factions in the states. In practice, this meant guaranteeing that the governments of the states have something to say about the formation of the central government and that they also have important areas of governing left to themselves. The main deviations from the Virginia Plan were in the selection and structure of the upper house of the legislature, the selection of the executive, and the grant of legislative authority to the national government. In each instance, the framers went just as far from the unitary form as they thought necessary to obtain adherence of state-centered politicians and then backed sharply away from going further.

[4] M. Farrand, *Records of the Federal Convention of 1787* (New Haven: Yale Univ. Press, rev. ed., 4 vols., 1937) Vol. 1, p. 21.

[5] For a demonstration of the *ad hoc* character of this federalism, see William H. Riker, "Dutch and American Federalism," *Journal of the History of Ideas*, Vol. 18 (1956), pp. 495-526, where it is shown that the framers' invention owed nothing, either positively or negatively, to the most well-known federalism then in existence.

The great debate, as every American school child knows, was over the representation of states in the national government. The essential modification that the proponents of the Virginia Plan were forced to accept was the equal representation of state governments in one house of the national legislature. The issue arose out of the fear of the nine small states that they would be swamped by the preponderant weight of the four large states. This was probably an unreasonable fear since the subsequent politics of the federation has seldom, if ever, seen the small states pitted directly against the large ones. Whether reasonable or not, however, the fear was real (possibly because the small states had generally been lax in their payments to the Congress whereas the large ones had not) and it led the small states to insist on some kind of equal representation. The large states acceded in order to keep the Convention in session and this modification rendered the states a formal part of the central government and ensured the retention of some of the federalism of the Articles.

Once the proponents of unitary government had made this one great concession, however, they were extremely loath to make additional ones. And it was this systematic resistance on their part that produced a federalism of an essentially different kind from the peripheralized federalism of the Articles.

Consider, for example, the way the framers handled the election of the executive, which was a problem with at least two dimensions. Given the traditions in the states, it was natural for the framers to suggest that the legislature elect the executive; but, since most of the framers were mild conservatives fearing too much authority in popularly elected legislatures, this natural method was undesirable. Given the existence of the federation of the Articles, the next most obvious method was election by some agency of the states; but, since the framers mostly wanted something approaching unitary government, state-controlled elections were also undesirable. Faced with this two-dimensional set of considerations, the framers had a terrible time. Twelve different methods of election were proposed, two of which were actually adopted in a preliminary way, before the electoral college was finally devised. Though this expedient was a poor one (for it had to be revised in the Twelfth Amendment and is still subject to constant criticism today), it satisfied them on both dimensions. From the point of view of the federal–unitary dimension, it is important to note that, however great the difficulty of decision, the proponents of unitary government managed to avoid giving the states a part in the process of election. Thus, having capitulated on the election of the upper house of the legislature, the proponents of centralism refused to capitulate further, even though the way out of their difficulty was hard to discover.[6]

Or consider, as a further illustration of the resistance of centralizers to peripheralization, the development during the course of the convention of the grant of legislative power to the national government. It started out in the Virginia Plan as the (previously quoted) unlimited grant. It reappeared just after the large states' capitulation on equal representation as substantially the list of the powers delegated to Congress by the Articles. Having capitulated on one thing, it appeared that the large states were capitulating on everything. But then revisions began to appear in debates and committee reports. For example, the first list gave the Congress simply the power to call the militia into its service. Then it was proposed to give Congress full authority to regulate and discipline the militia, which was then the only military force in existence and therefore of central importance to men who wanted a stronger central government for military reasons. This proposal failed quite probably because, as one delegate remarked, "If it be agreed to by the Convention, this plan will have as black a mark as was set on Cain." What resulted, however, was a compromise that allowed the Congress not only to call out the militia but also to "provide for organizing, arming, and disciplining" it and to govern "such Part of them as may be employed in the Service of the United States." This compromise, which seems quite weak to us today, was probably as far as the proponents of centralized government dared go, for, as it turned out, the militia provisions came under extremely heavy criticism in the ratifying conventions and the Second Amendment was tacked onto the Constitu-

[6] William H. Riker, *Democracy in the United States* (New York: Macmillan, 1953) pp. 146-49.

tion to ensure that the militia would never be fully transferred to the central authority.[7] For another example, the first list of delegated powers did go much beyond the Articles in that it enabled the Congress to "lay and collect" taxes. But in subsequent revisions this power was expanded almost into a general grant of power of the sort originally intended in the Virginia Plan by the addition of the phrase "to pay the Debts and provide for the common Defense and general Welfare of the United States." The meaning of this statement has always been ambiguous, for it is not clear whether the grant of power to provide for the general welfare is a grant for taxing or for all legislative purposes. The tradition of constitutional jurisprudence has been to assume the former, but the plain English of the sentence and the probable intent of the framers suggests that one ought to assume the latter. Under either interpretation, however, there occurred a considerable expansion of the power of the central government.

In short, the proponents of a centralized government made the concessions to federalism that they were obliged to make in order to keep the Convention in session and to offer a Constitution with a reasonable expectation of ratification. Beyond that they would not go and so resulted the centralized federalism of the new Constitution.

The foregoing description of the development of centralized federalism at the Philadelphia Convention of 1787 has demonstrated, I believe, the validity with respect to the United States of the hypothesis set forth at the beginning of this chapter. The military interpretation of the Constitution has demonstrated the existence of the military condition, whereas the determination of the centralizing framers to grant to the decentralizers only so much as was necessary to keep the convention in session and to produce an agreed-upon document demonstrates the expansion condition. In connection with the latter condition, I suppose it should be shown also that imperial expansion was impossible. It is conceivable that Virginia, Pennsylvania, and Massachusetts could have conquered some of their immediate neighbors; but no one thought of doing so probably because the cost would have been

[7] William H. Riker, *Soldiers of the States* (Washington, D.C.: Public Affairs Press, 1957) pp. 14ff.

thoroughly prohibitive. Hence there was but one means to centralize, namely to bargain rather than to conquer, and that is what the centralizers did.

The hypothesis has now been confirmed with respect to the first centralized federalism. It now remains to confirm it with respect to the eighteen other federalisms now in existence as well as the nine previous federalisms that failed. Space limitations prohibit a discussion of each of the 27 instances in the same detail as I have discussed the United States and, for that reason alone, I now relate the evidence from these 27 instances in summary fashion.

III FORMER BRITISH COLONIES AS FEDERALISMS

Over one-third of the federalisms existent today have been constructed by uniting former British colonies. Besides the United States, where the ex-colonials invented centralized federalism, Canada, Australia, India, Pakistan, Malaysia, and Nigeria started out as groups of colonies. Furthermore, some federalisms that failed were started under British auspices: New Zealand, British West Indies, and Rhodesia. Of the large British colonies now self-governing only the Union of South Africa and Burma have not at least tried federalism; and in both these instances there was considerable pressure from London to give federalism a chance. All these facts suggest that there is something in the British political tradition that is especially conducive to the federal form. And I am sure there is, although I have never been able to identify what it is in a way that is satisfactory to me. Those who are hostile to the British interpret their fondness for suggesting federalism as a part of the strategy of "divide and rule." That is, they interpret the imperial creation of semi-autonomous constituent units of a federalism as a means of generating internal dissension in the freed government, dissension that can be mollified only by recourse to the former imperial master. In connection with India especially, incautious Tory politicians actually uttered publicly statements of this "divide and rule" strategy; and such incaution has led many to interpret all ex-British federalisms as the last-chance frauds of a dying imperialism. But this view is, I think, too cynical. It supposes that the entire British policy on the treatment of lost colonies has been dictated by Machiavellian colonial officers; and I find such a supposition hard to believe. A more sympathetic view of the British imperialism is: (1) by using the system of colonial governors who were supposed to be absolute executives over a given area, the British effectively limited the size of colonies to what could be efficiently governed by one man; and (2) the area ruled by a governor was seldom, if ever, large enough to be a viable nation in the modern world. By granting, as a prelude to full self-government, provincial autonomy to the area ruled by a governor, the British created provincial interests which might reasonably demand continued existence and which the British (as the creators of the interest) might reasonably expect to recognize. In recognizing the provincial interests, the British were probably doing no more than displaying a sympathetic concern for their own creations. Though that may have been somewhat selfish, viewed from the standpoint of the colonial peoples, it is a far cry from "divide and rule." And in seeking to centralize by means of federalism, the British also displayed an altruistic concern that the self-governing units would be large enough to succeed in the modern world.

Regardless of whether the British penchant for federalism is a devious strategy for future control or simply a complacent assurance that their own colonial boundary markers were wisely placed, there can be no doubt that the penchant existed. Given its existence, one might suppose, therefore, that a sufficient reason for the existence of some of these federalisms is merely the pressure from the colonial office for its own favorite expedient. But such is not the case. As the following survey demonstrates, federalism in former British colonial territories has occurred in precisely the fashion set forth in the hypothesis at the beginning of this chapter.

Canada. Although the unification and self-government of the Canadian provinces, especially of the present Ontario and Québec, was discussed in the 1830's (following the minor rebellions in that era) and for a generation thereafter, no specific action was taken until 1864-67. It was precisely then that relations between the United States and Canada were more strained than at any time from 1777 to the present. As the Civil War in the United States drew to a close, outstanding Republican leaders discussed the possibility of annexing Canada, a process that would have been quite easy with the large and war-trained federal army. Going far beyond mere talk, however, the Fenian movement of Irish-Americans was organized to invade Canada. Its quixotic intentions were to promote a Canadian rebellion that in turn might, hopefully, lead to a war between the United States and Britain, out of which might come freedom for Ireland. In 1866 the Fenians actually did invade, quite unsuccessfully. Such is the backdrop in which after a generation of discussion the Canadians drafted and ratified a federal constitution in less than a year, a constitution the British Parliament substantially enacted as the British North America Act of 1867 in just one more year. Quite clearly, the second condition about the cognizance of a pressing military need holds in this instance. As for the first condition, it was clear from the reaction to the Durham *Report* (1839), which proposed the gradual elimination of French culture, that the unitary government Durham contemplated could be achieved only by force. The fact that the Canadian leaders never seriously considered the use of such force indicates that the expansion condition also holds in this case.

Australia. Although Australian federation has often been interpreted as a bargain made for strictly economic reasons (*i.e.*, inter-colonial free trade) and although there was no immediate threat of war when the union was consummated, only a slight survey of the circumstances of union indicates the omnipresence of the military–diplomatic concerns. Though some had agitated for federation from the 1850's onward, the federation movement really gained momentum in the early 1880's coincident with the French expansion in the New Hebrides. The first convention on federation in 1890, which was called because of a British military investigation that had recommended the unification of the colonial defense forces, also coincided with a frustrated Australian imperialism toward Oceania that had failed to maintain Queensland's annexation of New Guinea. But the most important event of all was the swift Japanese victory in the Sino-Japanese War of 1894, which resulted in Japan's annexation of Korea. With substantial imperial ambitions of their own and faced with a proven imperial naval power close by, the Australian colonials who could not agree on a federation in 1890-91 found it possible to do so in 1897-1900. Along with these direct military concerns stands the great diplomatic concern over Chinese exclusion, a concern which reached its peak in the 1890's and which was satisfied by an immigration act passed almost as soon as the new government was established. Thus, although the recognized military need is not so obvious in the case of Australia as in most others, military concerns were the ostensible reason for the federation movement and were probably crucial to its consummation.

As in the case of Canada, no thought was ever given in Australia to a unitary government. The self-governing colonial institutions were well established and easily able to resist unification, especially since the motive of defense was not desperately pressing. Hence the Australians substantially and consciously followed the American technique of the federal bargain.

India. Nowhere have the British more elaborately and consciously prepared their ex-colonies for federalism than in India. Throughout the entire period of British occupation of India, in fact, the British operated a kind of federal system in that they governed the provinces directly and the princely states indirectly. Thus the states stood in a kind of federal relationship to each other and to the rest of India. When forced to concede some degree of self-government, the form in which the British naturally chose to grant it was federal. The Government of India Act of 1935 suited the British purposes very well, for it granted self-government in those subjects of legislation reserved for the provinces and retained imperial control of those subjects reserved for the central government. Although Congress, the largest Indian party, refused to take office in most of the states, some Indian politicians were found to fill the cabinets of the states. Hence from 1937 to

1947, when the British withdrew from India abruptly, the states were operating governments with a conscious political tradition. Of course, also, the princely states had always maintained the fiction of self-government. Hence, although India superficially appeared to be a unitary empire, it, like Canada in 1865 and Australia in 1900, was a collection of partially self-governing colonies in 1947.

When Indian independence was granted, it came in the form of a partition of the subcontinent into India and Pakistan, a partition that occasioned the great rioting, vast transfers of peoples, and an undeclared war between the two new nations over the possession of the princely state of Kashmir and Jammu. From the very beginning, therefore, the Indian nation has faced the prospect of immediate foreign war, especially since Pakistan was more warlike, better armed, and more resentful than India of the boundaries drawn in 1947. As in the instances already mentioned, therefore, the Indian federalism, though foreshadowed by the Government of India Act of 1935, was actually entered into at a time of real threat of foreign war.

That the Indians chose federalism as a means of reconciling some subsidiary governments to centralization is demonstrated by the difference in their acceptance of federalism in the former provinces and in the princely states. Within a few months after independence, Sardar Patel had, in a whirlwind campaign, cajoled, threatened, bribed, and forced all the princely states into the Indian Union in such a way that most of them lost their identity. Of those which survived the first integration only one, Mysore, still survives a decade and a half later as a constituent unit of Indian federalism. Thus the Indians accepted, with some subsequent territorial revision, the provinces, which had had some experience in self-government and a well-developed local tradition; but they refused to accept any sort of federalism for the princely states, which lacked such experience. In the one case, the bargain of federalism seemed reasonable in the face of the threat of war; but in the other case, force was preferred to bargaining and the Union expanded by conquest rather than federalism. This choice is particularly clear-cut evidence of the existence of the expansion condition; and the widespread consciousness of the threat from Pakistan is sufficient evidence of the existence of the military condition.

Pakistan. All that has been said about the presence of the threat of war at the time of constitution-making in India applies with additional force to Pakistan. In the east, Pakistan is almost wholly encircled by India; in the west, one border faces India and the other faces Afghanistan, with which Pakistan has had perpetual though intermittent border warfare during its entire history.

But though the presence of the condition of recognized military needs is clearly confirmed in this instance, the evidence for the first hypothesis on federalism as the alternative to forced centralization is even clearer. After a prolonged period of constitution-making under an interim federal constitution, Pakistan adopted a kind of peripheralized federalism that, furthermore, under-represented East Pakistan. Shortly thereafter a military dictatorship was established, presumably to maintain the Union by force the better to face the Hindu enemy. What this experience indicates is that the federal bargain was indeed made to avoid the use of force, that the kind of bargain possible under the circumstances was inadequate for the military threat, and that it turned out to be necessary to use force to keep the central government militarily viable. Nevertheless the federal forms remain under the dictator so that, if he should no longer be necessary because the tensions with India lessen, federalism may again be used.

Malaysia. In Malaysia the British used the technique of indirect rule almost exclusively, except for the colony of Singapore. Since indirect rule involves the retention of local insititutions with puppet rulers, it amounts to an imperial version of federalism and indeed, when it was a colony, the British called this agglomeration of territory the Federated Malay States. This federalism was spurious, of course, for the puppets were indeed puppets; but it nevertheless conditioned the Malay peoples to an expectation of federalism.

Naturally, therefore, the Malays in making their first free government adopted a federal form. The military condition was present owing to the existence of communist guerillas, supported from China, whereas the expansion condition was present owing to the necessity of reconciling the previously federated states. Furthermore, faced with the prospect of Indonesian conquest of Borneo and outlying islands, the British engineered an expansion of Malaya into a genuine federation including Malaya proper, Singapore, and Borneo. The clearly discernible motive for this federalism was, therefore, a fear of Indonesian imperialism and a reluctance, on the part of Singapore, Borneo, *et. al.*, to accept Malayan domination. And this set of circumstances of course fulfills both conditions of the hypothesis.

Nigeria. Nigeria is the only one of the ex-British federalisms that does not display the unification of a number of separate colonies no one of which would have been viable alone. For most of its history under British rule, Nigeria had a unitary government. It was only as withdrawal became an immediate prospect that the British split Nigeria into three parts in anticipation of a future federalism. The justification for doing so was, of course, the existence of three geographically distinct and politically hostile cultures within the colony. The federal arrangements they made were highly peripheralized — subsequent political developments have peripheralized them even more[8] — and, owing to this peripheralization, it is surprising that the federation exists at all.

The only clear-cut reason — aside from the fact that the British prepared the way for it — that one can give for the continued existence of this federation during its first few years is the presence of Ghana and the pan-African (read: "imperial") propositions uttered by its leader, Nkrumah. During the time just before and during the Nigerian achievement of independence, Nkrumah's emphasis on pan-Africanism was at its height and no Nigerian leader could fail to be aware of the proximity of the western (and depressed and minority) region of Nigeria to Ghana. Nkrumah's personal pan-Africanism, that is, his personal

[8] According to John P. Mackintosh, "Federalism in Nigeria," *Political Studies,* Vol. X, pp. 223-47, the main political leaders prefer to govern the states and to send agents to the center, which is sufficient evidence of the highly peripheralized character of this federalism.

ambitions to unite at least West Africa under his leadership, seems to have diminished in the last few years and with this diminution the rationale of a federal Nigeria has diminished also. Only the future can tell whether this initial threat was sufficient to create a viable Nigeria federation or whether the peripheralization will culminate in dissolution.

Because of the peripheralization, Nigeria is a marginal instance; nevertheless the two conditions are verified for it: the second because of the Ghanaian threat and the first because of the unwillingness of Nigerian leaders to upset the bargain the British had made for them.

Unsuccessful British Federations. British colonial officials as a group never understood federalism. They failed to appreciate that the bargain is feasible only if there exists in all the prospective constituent governments both a sense of provincial integrity and a recognized need for military centralization. In their ignorance they have tended to organize federalisms on the basis of barely relevant considerations such as cultural diversity coupled with geographic contiguity. The Indian, Pakistani, and Nigerian federations, for example, were suggested on these bases, but came into existence owing to the presence of a military threat. Several other suggested federalisms, however, have failed to come to fruition largely because the British colonial officials have planned them on the basis of cultural or geographic diversity in the absence of military considerations.

Chronologically, the first failure occurred in New Zealand where, from the Constitution Act of 1852 until the Dominion's deliberate reversion to unitary government in 1876, a federal form existed. This federalism, of course, was based purely on geographic and communicatory considerations, on the distance between the north of North Island and the south of South Island. It was, however, a culturally unified society with no problems of foreign war, at least after the Maori had been pacified. Quite reasonably, therefore, the New Zealanders concluded that the federal bargain was both unnecessary and appallingly destructive of efficient government and hence abolished it in 1876.

Subsequent failures of British federalisms have come after

World War II, but the reasons for failure are similar to the instance of New Zealand. The projected, but abandoned, British West Indian federation was intended to unite the British Caribbean island colonies. But, though such a federation might have made a viable state in a way that no single island might, still the colonies felt no compelling military reason to unite with each other and hence the richer islands refused to take on the burden of the poorer ones. Again the federation of Rhodesia and Nyasaland, which was proposed on purely geographic grounds, broke down because the several parts feared different and conflicting military threats. Southern Rhodesia feared black pan-Africanism and Northern Rhodesia and Nyasaland feared white hegemony. Since the proposed constituent governments feared antithetical things, the federation had no basis for cohesion in a mutual military threat.

The moral of these failures is that federalism must be based on some deeper emotion than mere geographic contiguity with cultural diversity. Political sociologists like Deutsch (whose work is cited earlier in this chapter) are often inclined to accept a set of sociological preconditions as a sufficient reason for federalism. In these failed federalisms, however, all or most of the preconditions existed, yet the federalism never came off. So I infer the *necessity* of the political as distinct from the sociological conditions: Federalism is feasible only if both the conditions stated in the beginning of this chapter exist. In the instances of Rhodesia and the West Indies the first condition was absent; and in all three instances the second condition was absent. Hence these proposed federalisms collapsed.

IV EUROPEAN FEDERALISMS

Every national constitution originates of course in unique circumstances. The thesis of this chapter is, however, that the circumstances that have resulted in federal rather than unitary constitutions can be characterized by a recognized need for military–diplomatic unity and an unwillingness or inability of national leaders to impose centralization by force. Beyond these minimum characteristics, however, there seems to be little in common among the circumstances of origin of federal constitutions. In the previous discussion of federalism of the British Commonwealth, the origins showed additional common features: guidance from Britain and an adaptation of the main features of the United States' federalism to the parliamentary government encouraged by the British example. As we turn now to a discussion of the origins of European, Latin American, and other federalisms, this additional common feature disappears. One is again and again impressed that the only common feature of federal governments is that they are federal and that the only common features of their origins are the two characteristics the existence of which is here being confirmed.

Switzerland. The only survivor of the peripheralized leagues of late medieval and early modern times in Europe is the Swiss confederation. Yet it is not clearly a survival, except in popular tradition. The old confederation was replaced by Napoleon with a unitary Helvetic Republic and, although the Swiss returned to something of their old peripheralized federation after Napoleon's defeat, the desire for centralization, which the Republic had created, did not disappear. After several attempts, a reformed and centralized federal constitution, composed of elements of the old confederation and of borrowings from the United States Constitution, was adopted in 1848.

The old peripheralized confederation was formed at least as early as 1291 to resist the military encroachments of the Austrian Hapsburgs and served to maintain the political independence of the mountain cantons until Napoleon's conquest. This independence was, of course, far from absolute, for it existed only on the sufferance of the surrounding great powers, all of whom interfered frequently in internal cantonal affairs. In the period after 1815 such interference was increasingly regarded as offensive by Swiss nationalists and liberals, who espoused centralization as a device to minimize it. Their chance to centralize came at the end of the Sonderbund war, in which the liberal cantons defeated the so-called Sonderbund of conservative, Catholic cantons. The centralizers forced the liberalization of constitutions in the defeated cantons and then proceeded to reorganize the federation. Early in 1848 the conservative great powers (Austria, Prussia, France, Russia) forebade the constitutional revision; but owing to the revolutionary movement which swept Europe that spring, they were unable to interfere further in Swiss affairs. Hence followed the centralization of Swiss federalism in the Constitution of 1848 and, to an even greater degree, in the Constitution of 1874.

Both the old and the new confederations were therefore occasioned by the recognition of the need for military–diplomatic strength. But in neither the old nor the new was the desire for centralization strong enough to lead the centralizers to force a unitary government of the sort Napoleon had imposed. Even after the Sonderbund war the liberal centralizers wanted to conciliate the losers by retention of the federal form. So in the instance of Switzerland also the hypothesis is confirmed.

West Germany. The federalist tradition in Germany can be clearly traced as far back as the Confederation of 1815 and some say as far back as the Holy Roman empire. But the Confederation of 1815 was highly peripheralized and was used mainly as a device to frustrate liberal and nationalistic desires for unification. Hence the first appearance of something like modern centralized federalism came with the formation in 1871 of the German empire. Most commentators on the constitution of the empire have dismissed it as a "sham federalism." Nevertheless it displayed most of the characteristics usually mentioned in recent definitions of federalism: central and constituent governments each had unique and concurrent powers to govern the same people, guarantees of the integrity of constituent governments were given by the central government, and it originated in the circumstances of our two conditions. It was indeed more centralized than any federation up to that time had been, which is doubtless why it has been felt to be a sham; but it was considerably less centralized than subsequent federalisms with impeccable title to the name, and for that reason I have no reservations in asserting that it was the first German centralized federalism.

That the federation of 1871 originated under circumstances of great foreign hostility and was therefore aimed at improving the military–diplomatic position of the German states, especially of Prussia, can hardly be doubted when one recalls the Austro-Prussian War of 1866 and the Franco-Prussian War of 1870. Bismarck had pursued a policy of aggressive expansion and could expect hostility not only from those he defeated but also from those he threatened by his upsetting of the balance of power. His answer to this anticipated hostility was the consolidation of the peripheralized confederation into the centralized empire by means of the federal bargain. Bavaria, Baden, Württemberg, etc., were brought into the empire with a perpetual guarantee of their dynasties (the Kings of Bavaria and Baden, for example, were theoretically equal to the King of Prussia, except that he happened also to be the German emperor), with a second chamber to represent constituent governments (except that Prussia was by far the greatest government represented), and with a set of duties reserved to constituent governments.

Thus the federalism of the empire originated in exactly the circumstances set forth in the two conditions in the beginning of this chapter. Its internal arrangements were somewhat different from federalisms formed on the example of the United States in that almost all the legislative power was retained by the central government whereas much the greater part of the administration of both national and local legislation was delegated to the constituents. But this local variation, which Arnold Brecht called "horizontal" federalism in contrast to the "vertical" federalism of the American–Commonwealth tradition, may be ascribed to the unique circumstances of its creation without in any way denying the existence of the general circumstances common to all federalisms.[9]

Since the federalism of the empire, two new federal constitutions have been adopted in Germany, the Weimar constitution of 1921 and the Bonn constitution of 1949. Both have expressed the main feature of the imperial federalism; *i.e.*, its horizontal nature, and have thus not been "true" federalisms in the interpretation of legalists of the United States–Commonwealth tradition like Pro-

[9] Arnold Brecht, *Federalism and Regionalism in Germany* (New York: Oxford University Press, 1945) pp. 47ff.

fessor Wheare.[10] By their very continuation of this feature, however, they demonstrate that the crucial event in German federalism was the adoption of the imperial constitution.

By reason of the primacy of the imperial constitution, it is not necessary to show that the two conditions were present at the time of the adoption of the later constitutions. But to allay any doubts that may exist, I shall briefly show that they were present. In 1919, with the collapse of the empire, government in Germany substantially reverted to the constituent states of the former empire, which became republics in those troubled times. To organize a defeated Germany it was necessary to bring together again the constituents of the empire and this is precisely what the Weimar constitution accomplished in complete accord, therefore, with the two conditions. After World War II, constitution-making in Germany was dominated by American occupation forces who wished to impose federalism both as an alternative to the Morgenthau plan of Balkanizing Germany and as an expression of their provincial conviction that federalism was a "good thing." That the Bonn "fundamental law" was federal in nature may thus partially be attributed to the presence of Americans. But it may also be attributed to a deeper political circumstance: the hope and expectation of reuniting West and East Germany. What was written at Bonn was called a fundamental law rather than a constitution and was federal in nature because of the hope of attracting East Germany back into the federation. It was a proposed bargain in the face of the Soviet military threat and thus satisfies the conditions of the hypothesis.

Austria. As in the instance of Germany, centralized federalism in Austria appeared first in connection with the controversies in the 1860's over the nature of the peripheralized Confederation of 1815. Emperor Franz Joseph created the so-called Dual Monarchy of Austria-Hungary in 1867, after Austria's defeat in the Austro-Prussian War, as a device to strengthen the monarchy in its competition with Prussia for control of the German Confedera-

[10] K. C. Wheare, *Federal Government* (London: Oxford University Press, 1953) pp. 26ff. This is a characteristic example of Professor Wheare's provincialism in his fairly consistent misinterpretation of federalism.

tion. The Dual Monarchy provided for substantial local autonomy to the Hungarian aristocracy and, after 1873, provided some lesser measure of the same kind of autonomy to the Czechs. Thus the creation of the Dual Monarchy, which was a curious and wholly local kind of federalism, occurred in exactly those circumstances set forth in the two conditions. As in Germany, therefore, the federalism of 1867 provided the tradition to which all subsequent federalisms in Austria have adhered. But, unlike Germany, the federalism in Austria after World War I was not a replication of an earlier federalism. Rather it was based on the fact that, with the collapse of the monarchy, no governments were left in Austria but the provincial ones. As Schlesinger remarks, "Under such conditions Austria *was*, virtually, a federation (unless she was about to lapse into a state of anarchy) . . ."[11] Given the fact that some sections of even lesser Austria (by "lesser Austria" I mean what was left of Austria after the collapse and dismemberment of the Austro-Hungarian empire) were about to defect to Italy, the military–diplomatic reason for the federal bargain among quasi-independent provinces is abundantly clear. Thus the federalism of the first Austrian republic clearly satisfies the hypothesis. As for the second Austrian republic after the liberation of 1945, one can say that it repeated, under American auspices (perhaps one should say "dictation"), the institutions adopted after the World War I. And yet it too reflects something of the two conditions in a somewhat attenuated form. For Austria the main political events of the period between the wars were the attempt to create a unique Austrian nation and the failure of that attempt in Hitler's *anschluss*. Back of the federal bargain stands the fact of *anschluss*, the ever-present fear of an aggressive Germany, and, owing to that fear, the intention to give all parties and geographic areas a part in the government.

Soviet Union. The federalism of the Soviet Union, which is almost entirely indigenous, is as clearly the product of the two conditions as are the United States and German federalisms. The

[11] Rudolph Schlesinger, *Federalism in Central and Eastern Europe* (London: Kegan Paul, 1945) p. 253. See also p. 259, where Schlesinger remarks, "there could have been no alternative to federalism but civil war."

Russian revolution in February in Petrograd was accompanied by other nationalist revolutions elsewhere in the Russian empire so that the immediate end product of revolution in 1917 was a set of national governments in Russia, in the Baltic States, in Poland, in the Ukraine, in White Russia, in the Caucasus, in the trans-Caucasian region, and in central Asia. In some of these peripheral areas of the empire, such as the Caucasus, much the same sequence of events occurred as in Russia proper; that is, national revolutions were succeeded by left proletarian revolutions, whereas in others, such as the Baltic States, the national revolution was the end of the process. In Russia proper, during the period of civil war and war with Poland, Lenin sought to strengthen the Soviet government by the federal bargain with White Russia and some internal dissidents such as the Volga Germans. Thus he created autonomous units within the Russian Soviet Socialist Republic for the Volga Germans and later for the Kalmuks, the Bashkirs, the Tatars, the Kirghiz, the Daghestani, and the Crimeans. Autonomous governments such as these were clearly responses to the circumstances of the first condition; that is, they were a kind of bribe; but, since the dissidents conciliated did not necessarily feel any sympathy with the military objectives of the Soviet Union, these instances do not satisfy the second condition. But in the course of 1920–22 the left-wing governments of Armenia, Georgia, Transcaucasus, *et. al.*, all of which felt a genuine sympathy with the military objectives of the Soviet government in Russia, were persuaded to join with the Russian Soviet government. This juncture was formalized with the constitution of 1924, which joined Russia, White Russia, the Ukraine, and the Transcaucasus in the Soviet Union. It is true that the process of making this constitution started in 1922 and that by the time it was adopted the regional autonomy of the acceding governments had been abolished by means of Bolshevik domination of all the governments involved, but nevertheless when the process started the main governments involved agreed with Russia on military questions and gladly accepted the bribe of federalism to meet the military threat. Since 1923 the Soviet Union has been highly centralized and for that reason many scholars have refused to call it a federalism. This refusal is, however, merely the expression of the American–Commonwealth mythology that federalism ought to prevent tryanny. Since the Soviet Union preserves all the features of federalism, the mere fact that its federalism fails to prevent tyranny should not lead to casting it out of the class of federalisms. Rather it should lead to a re-evaluation of what federalism means and implies.

Yugoslavia. The federalism of Yugoslavia is based on three sources. One is the rather inchoate tradition of federalism from the Austrian empire; a second is the experience and example of the Soviet Union; and a third is the military–diplomatic ambitions of Marshal Tito. Apparently Tito attempted to use federalism for two purposes: (1) to satisfy resentful minorities within Yugoslavia and (2) to serve as an attraction to other Balkan states in the creation of a great central European nation under Tito's leadership. In the Austrian empire the Slavic minorities felt (and in fact were) oppressed. And when Yugoslavia was formed in 1919 as a kind of greater Serbia those same minorities, especially Croats, continued to feel mistreated. Tito's federalism was partially at least aimed at alleviating the sense of national oppression by giving territorially based ethnic groups some slight measure of self-government (or at least government by Communists from the same ethnic origins as themselves). Beyond this, however, Tito's federalism was constructed so that it might accept new members. Along with Dimitrov of Bulgaria, Tito had planned, with Stalin's approval, a Balkan Union, presumably to include both Bulgaria and Albania as well as Yugoslavia, perhaps to include Roumania, Greece, Hungary, and as Tito's ambitions grew, even Poland. At the same time Tito had plans to absorb at least Trieste and perhaps other areas of Italy and Austria. Federalism is an efficient form for such territorial expansion since new constituent units can be brought into the federation without losing either territorial identity or the jobs of their rulers.

In all the federalisms so far discussed (except possibly Germany, Austria, and Australia), the military need was to ward off or anticipate some expected aggression. In the case of Yugoslavia, however, the military need was imperialistic, for federalism there was clearly to prepare for aggression rather than defense. This seems clearly to have been the case also in the union of Ethiopia and Eritrea. But the variation in military objectives does not alter the fundamental relationship between federalism and military preparedness. Hence, although those prospectively imperial federalisms like Yugoslavia, Ethiopia, and possibly Australia and Austria and Germany initially may not seem quite the same as the rest, still these instances satisfy the conditions of the rather narrow military condition. And as prospective imperialisms, they also satisfy the expansion condition.

V SPANISH-AMERICAN FEDERALISMS

The essential features of the adoption of federalism in Spanish-American nations are so similar that these events can be considered together. All these federalisms originated in the military crisis of that prolonged and bitter warfare which seldom seemed to favor the revolutionists until near the very end. The wars started in 1810 and, at least in Bolívar's area (which was the militarily crucial one), were not completed until 1826. During that period Venezuela, Colombia, Argentina (including Uruguay), Mexico, and Central America adopted federal constitutions. Furthermore, for a short while Gran Colombia was a federation of what are now Ecuador, Colombia, and Venezuela. Thus, in 1826 much the greater part of Spanish America was governed by federalisms created during the course of revolution, presumably for the better prosecution of the wars.

An alternative interpretation of the motive for federalism in revolutionary Spanish America has nevertheless frequently been suggested. Federalism was often the rallying cry of the liberal parties, whereas conservatives as well as Rousseauesque military dictators like Bolívar and O'Higgins preferred unitary governments. Given this political division, it is easy to identify the movement for federalism as a movement for freedom. Thus, the origin of these federalisms can be interpreted as the adoption of a political ideal rather than, as I have previously interpreted it in every instance, as the adoption of a mere military–diplomatic expedient that is morally neutral.

Careful historians of Latin American thought are, however, thoroughly opposed to this romantic and idealistic version of the origin of Latin federalism. Speaking of "provincial sovereignty," Belaunde says:

> When the central authorities had been swept aside and the authority of the mother country was no longer recognized, the government fell necessarily into the hands of local oligarchies or of the *caudillos* who took the lead in the popular insurrection. So much for the fact. As for the doctrine, what we have is the logical result of the application of the principle of communal sovereignty when the Peninsular authorities had disappeared. This doctrine was exaggerated by Jacobin and federalist imitation.
>
> This is the true origin of American federalism . . . . In a general way, it is not badly applied ideology which created the movement or the tendency [*i.e.*, toward federalism] but the tendency supported by determined interests that encountered its ideology.[12]

In short, effective power, once Spanish authority was gone, lay in the hands of *caudillos* who were willing and eager to unite for revolutionary purposes but not for much else. This is, of course, the ideal setting for some kind of federalism, which in fact appeared over most of the former Spanish lands. That this interpretation is substantially correct is shown by the gradual disappearance of federalism once the pressing military need for it had disappeared. Chile prepared a federal constitution in 1826, adopted a highly centralized federalism in 1828, and abandoned federalism completely in 1833. Uruguay broke off from La Plata in 1828 and adopted a unitary government in 1830. In that same year Gran Colombia broke up into the constituent units of Ecuador, Venezuela, and New Granada (later Colombia). In 1839 the Central American Federation disbanded into Guatemala, Salvador, Honduras, Costa Rica, and Nicaragua. Finally, in 1886 the Colombian federation was revised into a highly centralized unitary government. So much for formal constitutional revision. In the post-revolutionary period, many federal constitutions have been operated (usually by dictators) as if they were unitary governments. Thus Mexico, for example, has retained a federal constitution through most of its history, although its federalism

[12] Victor Andrés Belaunde, *Bolívar and the Political Thought of the Spanish American Revolution* (Baltimore: Johns Hopkins Press, 1938) pp. 131-32.

has usually been as highly centralized as is the federalism of the Soviet Union. Only in Argentina and to a much lesser degree in Venezuela has the federalist tradition really survived — in both instances in a highly centralized form. The general interpretation of these events is that, once the fear of imperial reconquest subsided, the *caudillos* and local oligarchies had no motive to accept any kind of centralization. In some instances this changed state of mind led to the dissolution of the federation, whereas in others it led to centralizing dictatorships, some of which abandoned even the pretense of federalism.

All these remarks demonstrate that the second condition; namely, that the receivers of the federal offer be motivated by a military goal, applies to all Spanish American federalisms. And they demonstrate as well that the first condition also applies; namely, that the offerers of the federal bargain prefer federalism to conquest. When the concern over Spanish reconquest died down, federalism waned because few national leaders were willing to offer the necessary bargain to the *caudillos*. In those cases in which a strong national leader ultimately appeared (*e.g.*, Chile, Colombia), federalism was changed to unitary government. But when no strong national leader appeared, the federation simply dissolved into constituent units.

VI BRAZIL

It is customary to identify the origin of Brazil's federalism with the republican revolution of 1889.[13] But in fact the empire, like the later German and Austro-Hungarian empires, was itself a kind of federal government, the federal features of which originated in exactly the circumstances set forth in the hypothesis.

From the beginning there was a certain popular element in the Brazilian empire, an element epitomized in its very name, which was intended to recall the popularly acclaimed Roman *imperator* rather than a divinely chosen king. Furthermore, the heritage of Portuguese rule was decentralizing in character for the nation was from the beginning divided into coastal provinces,

[13] Herman G. James, *The Constitutional System of Brazil* (Washington, D.C.: The Carnegie Institution of Washington, 1923) pp. 1-8.

each of which acquired its own local traditions and ruling class. The original constitution of the empire was substantially unitary in nature, but in 1834 this constitution was revised by the Additional Act to create a kind of federalism, specifically a senate based on selection by provincial legislatures.

The immediate motive for the Additional Act was clearly military–diplomatic in nature. In the revolutionary deeds of 1831, Dom Pedro I had been expelled and the crown was given to his infant son, Dom Pedro II. In the ensuing year, partly as a reaction against the conservatism of the central government of Dom Pedro I and partly as an expression of the sense of independence of local oligarchies, there was a series of revolts in, especially, outlying provinces. In 1833 the constitutional revision of the Additional Act was proposed, chiefly to mitigate the conditions that led to the local revolts for provincial autonomy. This fact about its origin confirms the existence of the first condition that the bargain-offerers must prefer a bargain to conquest. In the next year, at just about the time of the passage of the Act, the agitation intensified for the return of Dom Pedro I, possibly with the support of European arms. Although the conservatives certainly did not intend this result, their agitation frightened the legislature into the passage of the Additional Act, with its federalistic reform of the senate, which theretofore had been the main source of conservative power. Thus the facts in this case also indicate the occurrence of the military condition that the bargain acceptors recognize a military danger. Subsequent elaboration of federalism in 1889 and later are simply continuations of the tradition established in 1834 by the federal empire.

VII NON-BRITISH FEDERALISMS IN AFRICA AND ASIA

These constitute a heterogeneous group of federalisms (Ethiopia, Indonesia, the Mali Federation, and the Congolese Federation), none of which is very strong, two of which have already failed, and two more of which have dim futures. Yet each in its way is an illustration of the validity of the hypothesis.

The strongest and apparently most stable is the Union of Ethiopia and Eritrea, which is a kind of dual monarchy. Each nation has its own constitution and owes common allegiance to the Ethiopian monarchy. This federalism is a joint consequence (1) of the United Nations' effort to divest itself of trusteeship responsibilities for former Italian colonies and (2) of the expansionist ambitions of the Ethiopian monarch. The UN sought a solution to its responsibilities and Ethiopia provided the solution with its federal proposal. This union satisfies the first condition in that Ethiopia was willing to offer the bargain as the only feasible means of acquiring the territory and it satisfies the second condition since for Ethiopia it was a means of imperial expansion in which Eritrea acquiesced. In this respect the Ethiopian federalism is quite similar to the Yugoslavian, the more so since the Ethiopian government may have envisioned the ultimate absorption of the several Somalilands (also under UN trusteeship) by means of the same device.

Mali Federation. In the course of the dismantling of the French empire, the French colonial administration, otherwise totally inexperienced with federalism, experimented with a West African federation, which finally ended up in attenuated form as the Mali Federation with a life of several months. The first French response to a realization of the probable success of independence movements was to propose the French Union; *i.e.*, the integration of colonies with metropolitan France. Since this was no more than disguised colonialism, it never caught on; but under the guise of assisting the Union, some West African politicians, notably the Senegalese leader Leopold Senghor, promoted a federation for exactly the same presumed motives of personal aggrandizement that Nkrumah has for promoting pan-Africanism. Although several other colonies were originally included, by the time of the formal independence from the French Community, only Senegal and Soudan were included, the one only fairly Europeanized, the other barely touched culturally by French rule. In the ensuing few weeks of federation, the main political question was the selection of a president. As the coalition-formation progressed on this point, it became apparent that Senghor would lose, whereupon he dissolved the federation.

It is notable that neither of my conditions was present in this federation. Senghor was eager to offer the federal bargain as long as he thought he could control the federation. Indeed, that the federation existed at all was owing to his previous willingness to compromise. But Senghor's eagerness disappeared when it appeared that federation would not suit his purposes. Thus the first condition was lacking. And no military threat existed at any time. The only military–diplomatic goal was Senghor's expansionism and this goal disappeared when the Soudanese outmaneuvered him. Hence the second condition was also lacking. In the absence of both conditions this federalism could not succeed.

Congo. The Belgian government, when it resigned from the Congo, left its colony with a unitary constitution. The civil wars that followed were at least partially occasioned by provincial resentment of the unitary form, although the attempts by Belgium, the Soviet Union, the United States, and the UN to influence provincial attitudes and decisions have so obscured the desires of the provinces that it is difficult to say what the indigenous peoples and politicians want. As a result of UN military intervention something of a federalism now exists in the Congo, based entirely for the moment on UN force. It is therefore too early to say whether or not this federal notion will survive or, if it does, whether or not it will remain a federation. In any event, the expansion condition is present by reason of UN insistence and the military condition is present by reason of the persistent intervention of Belgium and the Soviet Union.

Indonesia. The federalism in Indonesia, which was rejected after a substantial civil war, is especially interesting as an example in which both conditions of the hypothesis were absent. The rejection of federalism therefore suggests in a negative way the validity of the hypothesis.

Federalism in Indonesia was planned by the Dutch administration as a means of transferring power in all the Dutch colonies in southeast Asia. The core was to be Netherlands Indies (Indonesia) in association with Timur, Sumatra, Borneo, Celebes, Moluccas, New Guinea, etc. A sympathetic interpretation of the Dutch motives is that the Dutch colonial officials believed (1) that the cultures of the several parts were so divergent as to require considerable local autonomy if they were to remain together and (2) that federalism was an adequate device to guarantee that autonomy. On the other hand, a hostile interpretation of Dutch motives is that the Dutch believed that they might continue to play a significant part in Indonesian affairs after independence if those parts of the Indies still friendly to the Dutch had extensive autonomy from Djakarta. In this view a Dutch-imposed federalism is a form of the policy of divide and rule.

Fortunately, we do not need to speculate about Dutch motives for the significant fact is that, rightly or wrongly, Javanese leaders adopted the hostile interpretation. Hence they rejected federalism as just another piece of Dutch craftiness. Further, they rejected the entire notion of a bargain, preferring to use military conquest to acquire all reluctant parts of the Dutch Asian empire. Thus the first condition of federalism, the willingness to bargain, was absent. So also was the second. The Dutch colonial system had been founded on a remarkably small metropolitan base and persisted as long as it did only because of the military immaturity of the colonials. The effect of the Japanese conquest in World War II was to destroy much of the Dutch military strength and at the same time to educate the Indonesians. Simultaneously the German conquest of the Netherlands weakened the Dutch even further. It was therefore apparent in 1949, when the federal constitution came into existence and independence was proclaimed, that no serious military threat to Indonesia existed. Hence there was no need for a federal bargain and the second condition was not satisfied. Within less than a year (by August, 1950), federalism in Indonesia was abolished in favor of a unitary government.

Thus, Indonesian federalism failed simply because it could not satisfy the necessary conditions for federalism in its origin. The main historian of Indonesian federalism remarks in retrospect, however:

> Recent writers have rightly recognized that opposition to the federal state in Indonesia was largely due to the fact that it was

"Dutch-inspired" or "Dutch-imposed," rather than because of any absence of intrinsic merit in the plan.[14]

But in the interpretation of federalism set forth here there was indeed an intrinsic defect in the plan. I have been arguing that constitutions are bargains that come out of specifiable political conditions. Any attempt to copy a particular bargain outside of the specified political context is surely an intrinsic defect of the plan itself. And this is what was wrong with federalism in Indonesia.

* * *

On the basis of the evidence here set forth, we may conclude that the hypothesis is confirmed that the military and expansion conditions are necessary to the occurrence of federalism.

[14] A. Arthur Schiller, *The Formation of Federal Indonesia 1945-49* (The Hague: Van Hoeve, 1955) p. 9. Schiller cites George Kahin, *Nationalism and Revolution in Indonesia* (Ithaca, N.Y.: Cornell University Press, 1952) p. 450, in support of this view.

3

The maintenance of federalism: the administrative theory

Although a willingness to compromise and a recognized need for military unity are two necessary predisposing conditions for the federal bargain, they cannot have much to do with its survival. If they were the conditions of keeping the bargain as well as of making it, then remarkably few bargains would be kept. As military tensions eased, federal unions either would disintegrate or, if governed by determined centralizers, would become unitary. This is, of course, what happened to most of the peripheralized federalisms prior to 1787. And the few that survived for appreciable lengths of time (*e.g.*, the Swiss and Dutch confederations) were seldom without a dire military threat. Hence it may well be that the conditions necessary for keeping the bargain of a peripheralized federalism are the same as those for making it. But this surely cannot be true of centralized federalisms, for there are too many instances to the contrary. The United States has survived for a century and three-quarters, although the initial military conditions of its centralization disappeared within a generation after 1787. The Canadian federation has survived for nearly a century, yet the military–diplomatic concerns that called it forth were passing away even as the federation was founded. The Brazilian and Argentinian federations are both much more than a century old and yet the military dangers from both Europe and each other had disappeared by 1850. Etc., etc. It must be, therefore, that the conditions of keeping the bargain are different from the conditions of making it, at least in centralized federalisms. My concern in this chapter and the next two is to identify some of these conditions for survival.

In general the reason for the survival of centralized federalisms is the fact that they are centralized; that the rulers of the federation can overawe and overrule, but not annihilate, the rulers of the constituent units. Unfortunately a general statement of this sort is not very useful for it is almost a tautology. What one wants for understanding the survival of centralized federalism is a detailed analysis of the devices for overawing and overruling and of the devices for moderating the overawing; and such analysis can come only from surveys of constitutional arrangements. Such an analysis is undertaken in the following three chapters, of which I offer a preview here.

Survival has, as I have just pointed out, two features: (1) centralization, which allows the central government to exploit the advantages of a larger base for taxes and armies, and (2) maintenance of guarantees to the constituent units, which prevents the transformation of federalism to a unitary government. The most frequently offered explanation of survival attempts to combine these features with the administrative system. It asserts that the gradual transfer of administrative duties to the center provides for centralization whereas the sharing of these duties between the center and the periphery maintains the guarantees. In this chapter this assertion is examined in detail with respect to the system of federalism in the United States, incidentally presenting a fairly detailed examination of the way in which at least one federalism works. The conclusion of this survey is, however, that the administrative theory, though initially attractive, does not hold for the United States. Since it does not hold for the system for which and from which it was inferred, it probably cannot be expected to hold elsewhere. Given this conclusion, one must look elsewhere for an explanation of survival and hence in Chapter 4 I survey the institutions and cultural conditions in the United States that serve the centralizing and guarantee-maintaining functions. Having identified these institutions and conditions for one federalism, in Chapter 5 the same kind of institutions and conditions are identified in seven others. The main conclusion from Chapters 4 and 5 is that the structure of the system of political parties is what encourages or discourages the maintenance of the federal bargain.

I THE ADMINISTRATIVE THEORY OF FEDERALISM

Since the kinds of federalism have been distinguished by the division of areas of action between the central and constituent governments, the obvious way to investigate the degree of centralization is, according to the administrative theory of federalism, to look at the way in which the areas of action are in fact divided up. The traditional method is to examine the formal division in the Constitution and the gloss applied to it by judicial decision. (In most federalisms, courts interpret the exact meaning of the division; and in the United States it has been customary to refer to the Supreme Court as "the arbiter of federalism.") The fault in this method is that judicial decisions concern the boundaries of areas of action and do not in any way indicate their absolute size and importance. Yet most of the history and analysis of federalism has been written by constitutional lawyers using judicial decisions as their raw material. As a consequence the tradition provides us with a highly distorted picture of the relationship between the nation and the states.

In order to avoid the lawyers' distortion and to present the case for the administrative theory as fairly and completely as possible, one must look at the whole arrangement of authority over governmental functions,[1] which will be attempted in this chapter.

In order to survey the whole range of action in a systematic

[1] A step in this direction has been taken in Daniel J. Elazar, *The American Partnership* (Chicago: University of Chicago Press, 1962) which is an examination of the total picture of action by state and national government in several substantive areas. Unfortunately his picture is also somewhat distorted because of his avoidance of substantive areas not displaying the feature of cooperation he wished to emphasize.

way, we need some sort of distribution of functions into manageable categories. In Table 3.1 one possible categorization is set forth. It purports to be no more than a distillation of the common sense of the scholarly tradition about what governments in the United States do. Its usefulness, if it has any, is its completeness. And the test of completeness is: If some governmental action cannot be placed in a category except by an argument that scholarly common sense would regard as contrived, then a new category is needed and Table 3.1 is incomplete. If, on the other hand, and again in accordance with scholarly common sense, any given governmental action fits easily into one or more categories, then the table is complete. I have tested this table on a number of friends and, provisionally at least, I regard it as complete. Since it is offered only for the American tradition, however, it is clearly incomplete for others, although it probably fits the whole Western tradition fairly well. (Incidentally, it is not to be inferred that the categories are listed in order of importance for, quite obviously, importance varies over time and in accordance with unique historical events.)

Using this list, we now shall survey for each of the nineteen categories the division of action between federal and constituent governments from 1788 to the present.

II GETTING MONEY

Current Financing. The arrangements in the Constitution give almost unlimited taxing power to the central government, or so the first clauses of Article I, Section 8, have been interpreted in recent years. But given the kinds of taxes that had been invented in 1787 (*i.e.*, customs duties, excises on goods and services, capitation taxes, and taxes on real property), this grant is not nearly so generous as it appears. The right to impose excises, though granted, was not really expected to be used, as the response of the Whiskey Rebellion of 1793 indicates. Furthermore, the really productive tax was the one on real property, which the framers apparently intended to reserve for the states and localities by means of their confusing restriction on direct taxation by the central government (Article I, Section 9). By reason of wholly adventitious circumstances, however, this ap-

Table 3.1 FUNCTIONAL AREAS OF GOVERNMENTAL ACTION

A. *Getting Money*
   1. By current financing, *e.g.*, tax collection, sales of public property, etc.
   2. By deferred financing, *e.g.*, borrowing

B. *Spending Money*
   1. On external affairs, *e.g.*, military and diplomatic affairs
   2. On activities related to internal order
      a. Maintenance of public safety, *e.g.*, enforcement of criminal law
      b. Supervision of property rights, *e.g.*, defining and protecting ownership of realty and personalty
      c. Supervision of civic rights and liberties, *e.g.*, defining and protecting the right to vote
      d. Supervision of public and private morality, *e.g.*, censorship, supervision of marriage
      e. Inculcation of patriotism, *e.g.*, provision of national holidays
   3. On activities related to trade
      a. Provision and supervision of money and credit, *e.g.*, central banking
      b. Provision and supervision of facilities for transportation and communication, *e.g.*, management of the post office
      c. Provision and supervision of utilities, *e.g.*, management of wells and atomic energy plants
      d. Supervision and regulation of production and distribution of goods and services, *e.g.*, supervision of labor-management relations
      e. Encouragement of economic development, *e.g.*, granting subsidies
      f. Supervision of irreplaceable resources, *e.g.*, conservation and management of forests
   4. On activities related to citizens' welfare
      a. Provision and supervision of education
      b. Provision of aid to the indigent or handicapped
      c. Provision for recreation and culture, *e.g.*, maintenance of parks, musical societies, etc.
      d. Provision of public health services, *e.g.*, supervision of drug manufacturing
      e. Encouragement of the acquisition of new knowledge, *e.g.*, granting patents and copyrights, supporting exploration, encouraging scientific societies.

parently generous but actually niggardly grant of support to the center was soon augmented from another source: land sales. In its early years the central government subsisted almost entirely on excises and, especially, customs. But as the tempo of the westward movement increased, the income from sales of western lands outstripped all other sources of revenue. Indeed, it was possible for Jacksonians to lower the tariff largely because of surplus income from land — and it is not fanciful to suggest that the original Republican policy of free land and high tariffs were related: Once it started to give the land away, the central government was forced to rely on tariffs for revenue.

From 1815, the end of the second war with England, to 1865, the end of the Civil War, the Union was at its weakest. The British failure to invade successfully removed the threat of foreign war and thus removed one of the original conditions of federation. The failure of secession, on the other hand, ensured the continuation of the Union. But in between these two situations, the Union was weak. Quite probably one of the factors that allowed it to survive was the unanticipated income from land sales, which relieved the central government of the necessity for invading the states for tax purposes.

Until the second decade of this century both central and constituent governments could live on their traditional resources, although both kinds of governments, especially the central one, were forced to amazing contrivances in excise taxes. But the expansion of functions of government at both levels has forced the development of new kinds of taxes. The two major innovations have been the income tax and the sales tax, each of which has been adopted primarily by the kind of government best able to collect it. The crucial feature of the income tax is that the taxing authority must be able to collect on income earned in every place, lest capital flee from an income-taxing jurisdiction to one that is not. This the national government is able to do, especially since by currency control, etc., it is even able to collect on income earned outside the United States. The crucial problem of sales taxes is that the taxing authority must cover one territorial area completely in order to minimize evasion. This also the national government is able to do best, but the states can do it almost as well. Hence the nation has been the primary user of the income tax and the states the primary users of the sales tax.

I suppose there is no necessary reason why the income taxes should produce far more revenue than sales taxes, but such has in fact been the situation. On the basis of resources for current financing, then, the central government has come in this century to have far greater resources than the states. The Sixteenth Amendment (1913) was required in order to bring this situation about, although the authority granted was not extensively used until the 1930's.

Summarizing: In the beginning, states probably had better tax resources than the nation, although revenue from land sales made up for national tax disabilities in the first half of the 19th century. In this century, the tax resources of the central government have been much greater than the resources of the states, largely because of the decision to concentrate income taxation at the center.

Borrowing. As long as it was believed that borrowing by all levels of government laid a charge on future generations for the sake of the present one, the constitutional authorization of borrowing for the federal government did not place it in a special position. It was no more than similar authorizations to state governments for the purpose of spreading the payment for capital assets over the life of the assets. But when it came to be understood that borrowing by the central government had an economic effect quite different from that of borrowing by lesser governments, then the way was opened for huge expenditures by central governments even in peacetime.

The difference in economic effect between borrowing by the two levels of government is that borrowing by the central government is a cost to the society at the time of borrowing and is thus a kind of current financing like taxation, whereas borrowing by lesser governments is a cost to the society at the time of repayment and is thus genuinely a deferred charge. That borrowing by the government that controls the system of money and credit is only a current economic cost can be shown thus: If the central government with citizens $A, B, \ldots, N$ borrows x

dollars from citizens I, J, and K in time period t, no citizens (neither those in the set $\{A, B, \ldots, N\}$ nor those in its subset $\{I, J, \text{and } K\}$) can use these x dollars in period t. If the amount of money available for the private sector in the absence of borrowing is Q, then this amount for period t is $(Q - x)$. Thus what is borrowed diminishes the size of funds in the private sector during the period in which the borrowing occurs. When the central government repays x in time period $(t + 20)$, it taxes $A, B, \ldots, N$ to raise x and pays x out to I, J, and K. Since $\{I, J, \text{and } K\}$ is a subset of $\{A, B, \ldots, N\}$ there is no effect on Q. Hence there is no economic cost, but merely redistribution, in the repayment of x. It is quite otherwise with borrowing by lesser governments, especially if one assumes that the persons who lend are not citizens of the jurisdiction they lend to. If a state government borrows x dollars from non-citizens in period t, there is no diminution of Q for the citizens of the state. But in period $(t + 20)$, when x is repaid, taxes in x amount are taken from citizens to repay non-citizens, so that citizens have only $(Q - x)$. Thus the economic cost is incurred only when the debt is repaid.

Borrowing by the central government may thus be regarded as a kind of selective taxation in which the taxpayer voluntarily foregoes the present use of his money for the sake of interest. Furthermore, the interest is socially costless since it is merely a redistribution from all taxpayers to bond holders. As a tax that costs the society nothing beyond what the self-chosen taxpayer chooses to forego, borrowing by the central government is thus an exceptionally attractive tool of current financing. Since the realization in the mid-1930's that central borrowing had this feature, it has become a widely used tool of fiscal policy and public finance. In the United States, it has provided the central government with a potent new fiscal resource, partly at the expense of lesser governments. The framers of the Constitution specifically granted the central government the authority to borrow money, probably with the intention of ensuring that the debts to England (incurred by the treaty of 1783 to recompense for revolutionary confiscations of Tory property) would be paid. But because the advance of economic science has shown the fallacy of regarding all borrowing as a deferred charge, this simple grant of a traditional (but not heavily used) power has turned into a potent new kind of current financing—but only for the central government, not for the states and localities.

III EXTERNAL AFFAIRS

As I have previously shown, one immediately necessary condition for the federal bargain in 1787 was the presence of a severe external threat. Hence one of the main concerns of the framers was to improve federal control of military–diplomatic affairs. They did so by authorizing the central government:

1. to maintain an army and navy
2. to organize and use the militia of the states
3. to maintain diplomatic relations, to make treaties, and to regard treaties as part of the fundamental law.

We are so accustomed today to think of foreign affairs as exclusively the function of the central government that it is difficult to imagine ourselves back into the situation of 1788. Today this list of powers seems to be adequate to guarantee full centralization. But it was not so assumed in 1788. Not only were the states presumably to have some indirect control over ambassadors and treaties through the medium of the Senate, but the training and officering of the militia was directly in the hands of the states. Furthermore, the Second Amendment was intended to guarantee that state control of the militia would be reinforced and perpetuated.

It seems to me that, in 1788, even though the control of foreign affairs had been centralized somewhat in comparison with the situation under the Articles, still the control of this function was more peripheral than central. The grant of authority to the central government to provide and maintain an army and navy was initially only good intention, for neither existed in 1788. The only military forces in the United States, aside from one battery of artillery and several small coastal vessels, were the militia, which the states controlled. Furthermore, it was expected that the militia would make up the main, if not the only, military force for the foreseeable future. Or so, at least, I infer from some of the circumstances involved in the whole process of constitution-writing. Much care was taken at the Philadelphia convention to centralize the control of the militia to just the right degree. The framers as a whole would have preferred to nationalize, but dared not; and so they carried the process as far as they felt they could, producing a highly unmilitary division of command. Judging by the reaction in the ratifying conventions, the framers carried the process too far. In the Virginia convention, for example, more criticism was directed at the militia provision than at any other part of the Constitution. The result of this criticism was the Second Amendment, which perpetually guaranteed the right of states to maintain militia, presumably because they expected it to be the chief military force for the future. The significance of the retention of a major portion of control over military decisions in the states is that the grant of diplomatic authority to the United States was thereby severely undercut. The Constitution did indeed confide diplomatic affairs exclusively to the national government, as had the Articles; but the independence of the diplomatic negotiator is necessarily conditioned by the apparent validity of his threats and promises and this validity is in turn dependent on the military force behind him. Thus the fact that the American diplomat was deprived of the assurance of the American military force transferred even diplomatic decisions back to state capitols. As late as the War of 1812 this transference was clearly visible both inside and outside the nation. Altogether, therefore, the military–diplomatic provisions of the Constitution, though centralized in appearance, were in fact quite peripheralized.

Centralization in military–diplomatic affairs could not occur until the militia was replaced by the army and navy as the chief military force. The replacement occurred in the period between the War of 1812 and the Mexican War, largely because of the failure of the militia in the War of 1812. An army and navy had been created in Washington's first administration and under Adams the military acadamy at West Point had begun to produce officers. But all this was on a very small scale and the War of 1812 was necessarily fought mostly with militia. This disastrous war taught Americans some lessons: that the most successful units, that is, the navy, were the most professional; and that the militia was unreliable in open battle, as at Bladensburg, although it was adequate when entrenched, as at New Orleans. As these lessons gradually pervaded the American mind, the army and navy were expanded far beyond their prewar size, and the service academies produced (apparently deliberately) a considerable oversupply of officers. At the same time the states allowed their militia to decay: militia duty had come to be regarded as onerous, doubtless because of the battlefield failures of the militia, and democratic politicians naturally shrank from imposing an onerous duty on voters. By the time of the Mexican War only a few New England and Middle Atlantic states had a viable militia; and hence that war was fought with nationally organized volunteers.

Once the states abandoned their military arm, they lost their voice in foreign affairs, a loss that can be illustrated by the differing behavior of New England governments in the War of 1812 and the Mexican War. New Englanders of the locally dominant Federalist–Whig tradition disapproved of both wars. In the first one, their recalcitrance had actual military and diplomatic effect. By withholding troops they contributed to specific failures on the battlefield and by threatening secession they embarrassed and weakened the government in Washington, which was thus driven to conclude a hurried and unsatisfactory peace. In the second war, their recalcitrance meant only that New England was not a very good area for recruiting.

The final blow to state participation in the management of external affairs was, of course, the federal victory in the Civil War. Had the attempted secession, with all its concomitant negotiations with other countries, been successful, then the states doubtless would have retained a strong voice in external affairs. But secession was not successful. Indeed its main long-term effect was to generate a need for a strong federal army and otherwise to centralize decision making in Washington.

From time to time since the Civil War, the states have attempted to revive their militia. And today they are undoubtedly better than ever, although presumably much inferior to similar federal forces; but the revival has not affected the federal relationship and the states have never regained a voice in foreign affairs. The revival of the militia started in 1877, when the industrial states of the Middle West and the Middle Atlantic raised local forces to put down the first nationwide strike (in the railroad industry). As I have shown elsewhere, the growth of the militia in the next decade is highly correlated with the spread of labor unrest.[2] Since the National Guard, as it then came to be called, had primarily an internal police function, it could not and did not affect state participation in external affairs. In order to get some federal funds for their internal police, however, the states generally pretended that the National Guard did have a military function. And since there has been a high degree of interlocking between the officer corps of the Guard and local political party organization, the states have been able to persuade Congress to finance special Guard activities. But the federal army, which also has had a powerful lobby, has consistently resisted the military use of, especially, National Guard officers. The repeated outcome of the conflict between the two lobbies has been a compromise in which the states surrender some additional kind of control over the Guard in return for additional federal financing. If the states had hoped that they might regain military significance by recreating a functioning militia, the very form of the compromises has prevented them from doing so. Hence what the states lost between 1815 and 1847 they have never regained. The management of external affairs is exclusively in the hands of the central government.

IV ACTIVITIES RELATING TO INTERNAL ORDER

The initial and primary responsibility for activities in each of the five categories under this rubric lies with the constituent governments. Although by far the greater bulk of the work is done by the states, over the years the center has acquired some duties, especially in connection with marginal features, in these areas of action. Unfortunately for scholarly accuracy, the constitutional lawyers who study this control at the margin have given the impression that the federal government plays a larger role than it actually does.

2 William H. Riker, *Soldiers of the States* (Washington, D.C.,: Public Affairs Press, 1957) pp. 41-66.

There are two theses that I shall defend in the interpretation of the division of authority under this rubric:

1. It has been felt that duties in these categories are the function of the states.
2. When the central government has performed duties in this category, it has usually been assumed that such performance is either temporary or politically extraordinary.

Public Safety. This is the vast routine work of police and fire protection, criminal law enforcement (including the operation of penal institutions), and the mitigation of disasters, the great bulk of which is performed by state governments (and their creatures, the governments of cities and counties). The central government has, however, duplicated what the states do in the territory of the United States not subject to state jurisdiction. At times, indeed through most of the 19th century, this territory was large in area, though small in population. Some have suggested that the duties of the United States in fully governing initially the territory of states-to-be enhanced the national character of the Union and diminished state-oriented patriotism. But since central control of the territories was always felt to be temporary, it is unwise to force this argument very far. At most it can be said that the provision of internal order in the territories throughout the 19th century gave the central government something important to do at a time when its initially primary function of external relations had waned in significance. In the first half of the 20th century, when the United States was a minor imperial power, the central government was of course also responsible for the internal order of dependencies. But this responsibility too was regarded as temporary, as in fact it was. Further, since the United States had in this era much more to do than it had earlier, it is doubtful if the job of governing the Philippines in the 1920's contributed as much to the prestige of the central government then as did the job of governing Wisconsin in the 1840's. There is some territory, of course, which is assumed to be permanently within the jurisdiction of the United States alone, *e.g.*, the District of Columbia and permanent federal installations such as post offices and forts. These are regarded as extraordinary, however. Witness the persistent agitation to turn Washington, D.C., into something like another state. And the federal jurisdiction over special installations is regarded as an adjunct of other federal activities relating to external affairs and the regulation of trade. It is true that a federal criminal law exists for such territory, as well as federal prisons and special federal police (such as the F.B.I. and the Coast Guard); but all these permanent federal activities, though well-known, are but a drop in the bucket compared with the total maintenance of public safety by states and cities and counties.

The more significant federal activity in this area is, in contrast to the maintenance of order in territories, the supervision of order in the states. The Constitution requires the federal government to guarantee republican government in the states. But the federal government has made remarkably little use of this authority. By contrast with Latin American federalisms, India, etc., where a similar provision (copied, at least in the Latin case, almost directly from the United States) has often been used to centralize, the federal government in the United States has only infrequently intervened in the domestic affairs of states. Of course, the whole of Reconstruction after the Civil War constituted intervention, but the remarkable aspect of Reconstruction is that it did not set a pattern. Given the political situation of the mid-1860's—in which the central government was controlled by a party that had not yet won a national Presidential election by a majority—it is not surprising that Reconstruction occurred, nor is it surprising that it lasted ten years or until Republicans believed they could win without it. But this kind of intervention did not set a precedent, possibly because the basic situation of control of the central government by a party in the minority nationally has never recurred.

Lesser kinds of intervention have occasionally happened, usually at the request of state officials who find themselves unable to keep order, but occasionally over the opposition of state officials who sympathize with the disorder. Most such intervention in the past has occurred in connection with large-scale disputes between management and labor (from the railroad strikes of 1877 and

1893 to the steel strikes of 1952). Recently, however, most intervention has occurred because of the reluctance of officials of a few Southern states to subdue disorders occasioned by U.S. enforcement of U.S. court orders concerning civil rights for Negroes. In both substantive areas of federal intervention to maintain public safety and order, it has clearly been assumed throughout that the intervention is an extraordinary effort and is to be abandoned as soon as the crisis is over.

Except for the mitigation of disaster, which has come to be a recognized federal function provided the disaster is large enough, but which involves mostly financial aid rather than the maintenance of domestic order, federal intervention in this fundamental function of government has never been regularized. It does occur sporadically, but it is nonetheless assumed that domestic order is really the function of the states.

Property Rights. The maintenance of property rights, which is closely related to the maintenance of public safety, has also been traditionally assigned mostly to the states. According to the Beardian view of the Constitution, however, one of its main purposes was to centralize the control of property rights, especially to permit the national courts to supervise state legislatures and courts on this matter. It is true that several provisions of the Constitution do seem to have this effect, *e.g.*, the supremacy clause (Article VI, Section 2) and the prohibitions on states manipulating currency or impairing the obligation of contracts (Article I, Section 10). But the supremacy clause is a general grant of authority to central government, not limited to property rights as such, and is merely another feature of the centralized federalism invented at Philadelphia. And the prohibitions on devaluing currency and contracts, clearly aimed at a specific abuse common in the 1780's, was a prohibition on what was felt to be the business of the states, not a grant of power to the national government. To read these provisions as intending national control of property rights is simply another of Beard's anachronistic fallacies.

But, though the original scheme assigned this function to states (except that the national government was to manage currency and bankruptcy, two subjects on which variation among states is obviously unwise), still the nation does now partially govern property directly because of two main developments: (1) the emergence, in the post-Civil War period, of the Supreme Court as a really powerful maker of national policy; and (2) the acquisition by the national government of great responsibility for the soundness of the economy. The latter development, which will be considered later in the chapter, inevitably invested some control over property rights in the center. The former development, which came about as a basic structural change in the system, will be considered here. From the very beginning some judges on the Supreme Court aspired to make policy, especially in this area, for the whole nation. But they were successful in only a limited way until after the Civil War, at which time the judges' personal motive of aggrandizement coincided with a national conservatism. The first major attempt by the Supreme Court to define property rights was abruptly rebuffed: the Court entertained a suit by a citizen of one state against another state for alleged denial of property rights and the Constitution was promptly amended to deny the Court jurisdiction in such suits (Eleventh Amendment, adopted in 1798). Soon thereafter John Marshall, who is usually described as the great centralizer, came to lead the Supreme Court. But Marshall's centralization consisted chiefly of the enunciation of decisions that had little practical effect in their own time and are important today chiefly as precedents for a later centralization. (The lawyers' overemphasis on Marshall's work has been one of the main anachronistic distortions of the development of American federalism.) Marshall's main effort to supervise state control of property rights in the *Dartmouth College* case (1819) in which the Court held that a charter, as a kind of contract, could not be directly revoked by a state. The main effect of this case was, of course, to induce state legislatures to insert a revocability clause in all subsequent charters. And Marshall's successor, Taney, who had less reason to aggrandize the Court since he represented the leading party, restricted the effect of the case even further. The Supreme Court in the pre-Civil War period was a far less significant body politically than it subsequently became and hence it could not, even though some judges wanted it to, supervise property. In the era of the Civil

War, however, the nation acknowledged the right of the Court to declare acts of Congress and the President void and this acknowledgement raised it to a new level in the system. One of the things the judges did with their new power was to supervise the substantive due process of acts of state legislatures and regulatory agencies. (Due process, once merely a protection of procedural fairness in court proceedings, was expanded in this era to mean fairness of the law or order under which the proceeding was initiated.) From the 1890's to the 1930's the Court made basic rules on property by means of this device. Since 1938, however, the Court has refused to use this doctrine to regulate property and this self-denial may constitute a basic regression in the over-all tendency toward centralization. Nevertheless, that control of property which came as a result of federal management of the economy has increased rather than abated so that the Supreme Court's self-denial may now be quite insignificant in the total view of federalism.

In summary, the control of property rights lay almost exclusively with the states until after the Civil War. By the 1890's the Supreme Court began to set some basic guidelines. Somewhat earlier the central government had begun to regulate the national economy, incidentally thereby regulating property in a basic way. Today the former activity is abated but the latter has regularly increased. The consequence is that today the maintenance of property rights is a shared activity. In my opinion, however, the states are dominant — for they define and regulate the ownership of both realty and personalty — but the federal government has now a significant role at the margin (*i.e.*, on some contested questions).

Civic Rights. These too have typically been regarded as the responsibility of the states. Until recently, only the right to vote has been significantly regulated by the national government. And even this regulation has taken the form of setting the boundaries of the policy of the states. In two amendments to the Constitution, the nation has stated that the states may not deny the vote to persons on account of color or sex. But it has set no positive standards. Indeed, it has shied away constantly from setting positive standards because, I assume, these are felt to be exclusively the province of the constituent governments.

In recent years, however, the central government has invaded this area more than any others under this rubric, again largely because of the aggrandizing tendencies of the Supreme Court. Throughout most of our history the Court had no rationale with which to supervise the states in this area. The first ten amendments, concerned as they are mostly with civil liberties, might be supposed to grant control of them to the central government. But in the case of *Barron v. Baltimore* (1833) it was held that these amendments regulated *only* the central government, not the states. (Incidentally, it was Marshall, the supposedly great centralizer, who wrote the opinion in this case.) Not until the 1920's did the Court find a rationale to insert itself in these matters, when it held that the due process clause of the Fourteenth Amendment applied some of the civil rights protections of the first ten amendments to the states. Gradually, in the last generation, the Court has undertaken to regulate states in these matters to a greater and greater degree. On the whole, the states have acquiesced. Today we have reached this point: The setting of the boundaries and many of the definitions of civil rights are now a function of the center; the day-to-day enforcement is a matter for the states; but on dramatic occasions the United States enforces also.

Public and Private Morality. Although the liberal tradition has always denied that private morality is of any concern to government, the fact is that governments have invariably regulated such matters as marriage, sexual behavior, the use of stimulants, sacrilege, etc. In our tradition the states fully control these things, although the Supreme Court sometimes has become peripherally involved via the full faith and credit clause (Article IV, Section 1). In exceptional instances the United States has indirectly controlled (*e.g.*, by refusing to admit Utah as a state until it prohibited polygamy and by prohibiting the insterstate transport of women for prostitution). The one great instance of direct federal control was the Eighteenth Amendment, which, however, was not passed until most of the states had themselves prohibited the sale of alcohol. The fact that this matter was handled by a constitutional amendment indicates the prevailing belief that the regulation of morality was believed to be basically a state matter.

Patriotism. Probably all levels of government have felt called upon to inculcate patriotism. Since the objects of inculcation are mostly children, the states with their function of education probably have the greater responsibility. On the other hand, the military forces are very much involved in patriotic displays and the inculcation of patriotism in young men.

V ACTIVITIES RELATING TO TRADE

Money: Currency and Credit. Although the Constitution gives exclusive control of currency to the central government, one of the persistent political conflicts for well over the first century of this federation was whether the states or the nation would control credit, the more important form of money. The great controversy between Jefferson and Hamilton started over the chartering of the first Bank of the United States. Marshall's most famous pronouncement on national authority was uttered in *McCulloch v. Maryland* (1819), in which a state tax on the business of the second Bank was held void. And Jackson separated the Democrats and Whigs by means of the controversy over the rechartering of the second Bank. After Jackson it appeared that the states had won, but in the next generation the United States again developed a national banking system, without, however, a central bank.

A central bank, the Federal Reserve System, was established in 1913. And in the 1930's the remnants of the state banking system were brought under some federal control by the Federal Deposit Insurance Corporation and other specialized banking agencies. Though the dispute over banking has not always been couched directly in terms of the centralist–peripheralist dichotomy (Jackson, for example, fought the Bank as a private monopoly under government auspices), still the ultimate significance of the dispute has always been the effect on centralization. The issue is, of course, whether or not the federal government can use the banking system to try to control the basic course of trade. (The converse is not in question, however, for a state-managed banking system cannot control anything, least of all itself.) The history of the issue in the United States is simply that initially Hamilton asserted the power for the federal government, that his opponents triumphed in the next generation, and that in this century under Wilson and Roosevelt the control of banking has been vested mainly in the central government.

Transportation and Communication. Like money, facilities for transport and communication are basic instruments for trade; and throughout recorded history, governments, once strong enough to maintain external self-control and domestic order, have turned to the promotion of these instruments as a means of promoting trade. In the tradition of the United States, where external problems were minimal from 1815 to 1941 and where domestic order has not been hard to keep except from 1861 to 1865, the function of encouraging trade has been a major duty of governments at all levels. It is a paradox of American capitalism that, although private industry has accomplished more here than anywhere else in the world, governments here have also promoted private industry more than anywhere else in the world. Much of this promotion has come in the guise of providing facilities for transport and communication.

The usual rule (not always followed, of course) for the division of labor on this function among the several levels of government seems to have been: The smallest government that rules both terminals of the proposed line of transport or communication is the one to promote and supervise it. The operative effect of this rule is that initially the states were the main promoters, whereas in the last century or so the United States has become the main one. Even in the beginning, however, the central government had quite a bit to do and today the states have quite a bit to do. At no point is there an exclusion of one kind of government from the function. Rather, the function is fully shared. It is just that the recognized rule of division gave the states the preponderance of the task in the beginning and now gives the preponderance to the nation.

The usual rule (again not always followed) for the division of labor between private enterprise and the appropriate level of government (chosen according to the previous rule) has been: If the appropriate political authorities believe the line is justified by prospective needs of trade, then the line is built either (1) by a private capitalist under government supervision if a capitalist can be found to provide enough funds and to bear the risk, or (2) by a private capitalist under such subsidy and supervision from the appropriate government as is necessary to make him willing to bear the risk, or (3) by the appropriate government itself, especially if the amount of capital necessary is greater than most private organizations have.

What has resulted from these two rules is a very mixed system with elements of private enterprise (usually supervised by a government) and elements of governmental enterprise from village to nation.

In the beginning the central government ran the post office and supervised coastal shipping. States and localities maintained the road system, bridges, and ferries (often chartered to private entrepreneurs), and ports. As the nation expanded the main avenues were turnpikes and canals, which reached their zenith in the 1840's and 1850's. Except for the National Road and some small canals, the road and canal building was done by states. Even then the Corps of Engineers was improving navigable waterways, but still the system of water transport largely depended on state initiative. With the coming of the railroads, especially the transcontinental railroads, the balance of endeavor swung to the national government. Though the states subsidized and authorized many railroads in the East, the great subsidization was the federal land grants to western lines. Of the western states, only Texas made grants as large, in proportion to its size, as the United States. The federal authority over the railroad system was officially recognized with the establishment of the Interstate Commerce Commission in 1887. The railroads drove the canals out of business, but water transport survived on natural inland waterways, which were the child of the federal government also. By the end of the 19th century, however, the preponderance of effort in providing transport facilities had shifted from the states to the nation. In the ensuing few decades, it initially appeared that this relative weight might shift back again owing to the development of the automobile and truck, for which states provided paved roads. But it turned out eventually that states were not financially competent to provide all the roads necessary for this kind of transport. Gradually the United States has undertaken to control more and more roads, even in cities, so that today the road system is almost as much national as state. Something of the same thing happened with airlines, the initial subsidies for which (*i.e.*, airports) were provided by states; but as the business expanded, federal subsidies and control far outweighed state support and regulation.

With respect to communication, the post office has always been national and so has most of the subsidy and control of telegraph and cable communication. Telephone communication, however, which is primarily local in nature, has been subsidized and regulated mostly by states (except for interstate traffic) — a fact that is recognized in the structure of the subsidiaries of the American Telephone and Telegraph Company. Radio and television, which are interstate in structure, have been regulated and subsidized from the very beginning by the central government.

What this survey indicates is that all kinds of government have something to do with promoting traffic. Often the same industry, *e.g.*, telephone, is regulated and subsidized extensively by both levels of government. The present state of supervision of transport and communication can be indicated by Table 3.2.

Table 3.2 Supervision of Transportation and Communication

Industry	*Primary provision or supervision*	*Substantial secondary provision or supervision*
Road transport	states	United States
Railroad transport	United States	states
Inland waterways	United States	. . .
Marine transport	United States	. . .
Air transport	United States	states
Mail	United States	. . .
Telephone	states	United States
Telegraph	United States	. . .
Radio and television	United States	. . .

Utilities. Utilities have always attracted government supervision. Like transport facilities, utilities have a public character, for it is believed conventionally that they should be provided to everybody and that the market and exchange method of allocating resources does not guarantee such provision. Hence, presumably, political allocation is necessary.

Much the same rule for the division of the labor of allocation has been followed here as in transportation, *viz.*, if the area served by a utility is wholly within a state, it has been promoted and subsidized by states; if not, then by the central government. Until quite recently most utilities were necessarily local and hence were provided locally and supervised on a state level. Thus, the provision of fresh water, the disposal of sewage and garbage, the provision of warehouses, stockyards, grain elevators, and the like, and the provision of water power, electricity, gas, and heated air have been performed either directly by local governments or by private entrepreneurs under close state and local supervision. Only in this century has the United States entered the field in a significant way: (1) by promoting and regulating irrigation systems derived from interstate rivers, (2) by supervising and financing sewage disposal in interstate rivers, (3) by generating electricity and selling it on an interstate basis, (4) by financing rural electric cooperatives, and (5) by regulating interstate transport of gas and electricity. All of these activities are, however, simply supplemental to the task done by the states.

Regulation of Production and Distribution. Despite the supposed American adherence to economic liberalism, those who have been dissatisfied with the operation of the free market have repeatedly sought to modify market outcomes by political bargains. Regulation of wages, prices, working conditions, apprenticeship and entry into trades and professions, conspiracies to restrain trade, monopolies, etc. have, therefore, been a regular part of the functions of American governments at various levels throughout our history. The decision about which level of government should modify the market outcome is, of course, a practical one, entirely dictated by the size of the market. Until quite recently, the market for bread, for example, was entirely local, so that the regulation of bread prices, bakers' wages, etc. was undertaken by local, or, at the largest, state governments. But the market for wheat and flour has always been larger than individual states so that it has only been regulated successfully by the central government. Thus it is that in the early period of our history, indeed until nearly the end of the 19th century, most markets were local and hence most direct regulation of the economy was local also. But the vast technological changes in transportation have rendered most markets, at least most markets for goods, national. So, gradually, the regulation of market outcomes has become a national function, especially since the 1930's.

But not, of course, without intense resistance. Each act of regulation modifies a market outcome in such a way that one set of persons gains more than the market would give it and another set loses something it might otherwise have. Those who lose by regulation of course resist and, in our circumstances for the last 75 years, their resistance has taken the form of denying the central government the right to regulate the market.

In this struggle the Supreme Court for about 50 years after 1890 sided with the losers from regulation and did nearly everything in its power to prevent national regulation of markets. It systematically weakened the effect of national antitrust laws. By defining "production" as something distinct from commerce, it interpreted the federal authority to regulate commerce as a mere grant to regulate transportation. It limited the plainly unlimited federal authority to tax to merely taxation for support of those substantive functions otherwise granted. Thereby it rendered national regulation of markets almost impossible. The older commentators on constitutional law interpreted this policy as a preference for laissez-faire economic theory; but this, I believe, grants more philosophical sophistication than the narrowly trained lawyers on the Court then possessed. The main argument of those who attribute motives of theory-realization is that simultaneously the Court also restricted state and local regulation of markets by means of the due process clause of the Fourteenth Amendment. The effect of these simultaneous restrictions on both kinds of government, a restriction that E. S. Corwin called "dual federalism," was that markets could not be regulated by any government, state or national. And this result is, of course, what economic liberalism demands. But to a later generation this coincidence of theory and practice appears purely accidental. It seems more likely that, having excluded national regulation of national markets out of a straightforward partiality for the people who would lose by regulation, the business-oriented lawyers on the Court recognized that local regulation of a national market would entail a disastrous relocation of industry and so simply saved states from the consequences of their own folly in attempting to regulate national markets. Whether philosophically or practically inspired, however, the fact is that for about 50 years regulation of national markets was rendered very difficult by the Supreme Court — and at a time when most markets were becoming national.

In the long run the potential losers from regulation; *i.e.*, chiefly traders from Wall Street to Main Street and mine and mill owners everywhere, could not hold out in a democracy based on "one-man, one-vote" against the much more numerous class who expected to benefit from modifications of the market; *i.e.*, the vast number of farmers who sold their produce to traders, the vast number of laborers who sold their services to entrepreneurs, and, under another aspect, the vast number of small-scale entrepreneurs who bought from semi-monopolistic producers. The dramatic conflict in 1937 between President Roosevelt and the Court, which resulted in a defeat for the President in his proposal to revise the Constitutional structure and in a victory for the President (by reason of the resignation of one judge and the self-reversal of another) over the Constitutional doctrine, was the beginning of the acceptance of national regulation of national markets. In that confrontation the Court backed down on the doctrinal issue to save its structural integrity and, as result of this outcome and the subsequent appointment over the next 25 years of judges sympathetic to national regulation, all the legal barriers to national regulation so carefully erected in the two generations before 1937 have been swept away. As might be expected, those who lost the legal battle have continued to fight a political one, but their heart has not really been in the struggle. The nation has been extraordinarily prosperous since 1937, perhaps because of these very modifications of market outcomes, perhaps because of adventitious factors, and this very prosperity has come to those who lost as much or more than to those who won. Naturally the losers have been reluctant to upset a system in which they win along with everybody else.

As a consequence, numerous markets are now federally regulated without much objection: many markets for agricultural commodities are directly regulated from the supply side and, in some, prices are fixed by executive action; the supply of labor has been regulated by the National Labor Relations Board and the price of labor has been almost directly regulated in numerous crisis instances in basic industries (such as railroads and steel) by executive action at the Presidential level; federal anti-monopoly legislation (with respect both to mergers and to direct conspiracies to set prices), which was originally enacted in 1890 and 1914, has been enforced generally for the first time in the 1950's and 1960's; securities markets have been regulated in detail since the 1930's; price maintenance by local retailers (a market modification to protect local retailers operating in a national market) usually has been enforced for the last generation; minimum wages and maximum hours have been set in an increasing number of markets since 1938; etc., etc. There is no necessary economic coherence in this regulation. Anti-monopoly legislation does not jibe with retail price maintenance, for example. But there is a political coherence in it all; namely, those who have sufficient political influence to bring about a market modification in their favor have done so — and they usually have done so through the medium of the central government with its present-day control of national markets.

This is not to say that significant markets are not still controlled by states. Indeed they are. When the supply of a commodity originates chiefly in one state, it is possible to control market outcomes by controlling production. Thus Texas can control gasoline prices and California can control the prices of certain fruits. All states regulate the building industry minutely and the function of supervising local markets lies chiefly with states. Most markets for services are state-supervised. The ambiguously named U.S. Employment Service is partly financed by the federal government but is operated and largely controlled by the states. Licensing of trades and professions, which is really a control of entry or supply, is under state regulation: *e.g.*, accounting, barbering, bricklaying, engineering, hacking, law, medicine, plumbing, teaching, etc., are all licensed trades or professions, the entry to which is still state-controlled. In a number of these the prices of services as well as entry are also state-controlled. But only the most local of these are really state-controlled — the professions, as distinct from the trades, tend to be national in character so that states lose control by competition with each other, and as a result regulation is self-defeating and is eventually abandoned.

On the whole, markets are national nowadays and hence economic regulation or the modification of market outcomes is national. And this is a remarkable change from the 19th century.

Economic Development. This function, unlike the one just discussed, is not necessarily tied to the nature of markets. Even when a market is completely national, a state may seek to aid its citizens in the market by helping them to produce more cheaply or more efficiently. Thus states have subsidized much agricultural research, pest control, etc. State universities have had research institutes added to them to serve local industry. In the mid-19th century, most states had geological surveys, the better to exploit land resources, etc., etc. Furthermore, when markets are national the location of producers is partially undetermined. States can, in such circumstances, affect the location of industry to their advantage by offering subsidies to producers. Of course, this kind of bidding can become self-defeating if all states participate; but so long as some are less active than others in subsidization, it continues to go on. Throughout our history states have subsidized entrepreneurs: initially mostly in transportation, but in this century in nearly all kinds of business.

Substantial as commercial research and subsidies by states are, still the United States has spent far more than the states during the last generation, even if one omits the field of transportation. (And of course throughout our history the protective tariff has been a national subsidy to selected industries, a subsidy that, however, has not directly cost the government.) There is no single reason why direct subsidies to producers have become a national function, except perhaps the fact of superior national resources in recent years. Some subsidies, *e.g.*, to shipbuilders and mineral producers, have been justified on military grounds. So also have the vast contracts for weapons development and space research, although in practical effect they are subsidies to aircraft, electronics, and similar industries. Entirely aside from the militarily justified subsidies, however, are subsidies to and research for agriculture, not in the interest of market regulation, but in the interest of greater productivity. Partly these are justified by the nature of the problem; corn borers, for example, do not recognize state boundaries. Partly, however, the central government deals with these problems simply because it and they are there. Something of the same may be said about subsidies like cheap credit for small business. Any level of government could handle this function, but the federal government does, partly because it has the money, partly because it is there. The census function, originally purely political in nature, has expanded into a business service and by example has spawned numerous data-gathering activities in the Commerce and Labor Departments. There is constitutional justification for the census, but many of its duties are assigned simply because it is there.

Irreplaceable Resources. In the field of conservation, which has been a governmental function only in the 20th century, much the same principle holds as in other areas discussed under this rubric: If the resource to be conserved can be protected by state action, then the function is assigned to states; if it cannot be, then it goes to the central government. Since much so-called conservation is really covert regulation of a market and since most markets are national, it follows that most conservation is also a national function. Soil, uranium, forests, wildlife, and gas and oil are the chief regulated resources. Of these, only oil is fully regulated by a state (and this is, of course, simply market regulation from the supply side, a regulation possible only because of the large concentration of oil in Texas.) States participate in forest conservation and may even exceed the efforts of the United States in wildlife conservation. In sum, it appears, however, that the central government probably does more conserving than do all the states combined.

VI ACTIVITIES RELATING TO CITIZENS' WELFARE

Education. Traditionally, education is the business of states and localities and it remains so today. There always has been, however, a substantial amount of federal aid indirectly and at the edges of the system. From 1787 onwards most federal arrangements for the sale of public lands have reserved some proceeds to support schools. During the 19th century the service academies formed a larger part of the system of higher education than they do today. Vocational education has been subsidized by the United States since 1917. Much educational research is done by the U.S. Office of Education. Children's lunches have been provided since 1946. National fellowship programs for graduate education are simply a regularization of subsidies given for research (by various scientific agencies such as the Public Health Service) but actually used to support graduate students. Grants to support schools in areas significantly affected by federal installations have been given since World War II, and recently the federal government has subsidized dormitory building for colleges. But these varied grants (most of which, in recent years at least, have been compromises resulting from the failure of a general aid to education bill) are all on the edges of the system; they do not involve any significant federal control of education at any level. The states are still in control of education.

Aid to the Indigent and Handicapped. In the American tradition, poor relief has traditionally been associated with local government, probably because the preceding way in which society handled the function — through the parishes of an established church — was also specifically local. Today, however, the function is thoroughly shared by the nation and the states, with the United States bearing by far the greater portion of the cost and labor. On their own initiative and at their own expense, the states still do much of what they have always done, *e.g.*, they operate hospitals and asylums. With the assistance of federal funds and usually with federal supervision, states continue to do (often in new ways) many traditional functions, *e.g.*, supporting widowed, orphaned, handicapped, and aged indigents. Under the fairly close supervision of the United States, the states operate the unemployment insurance program. But the really large welfare program is Old Age and Survivors' insurance, which is operated entirely by the United States.

The history of the development of federal participation in poor relief begins with a series of quite modest grant-in-aid programs for special welfare problems involving women and children, as well as a pension program for railroad employees. These began in the second and third decades of this century. Had there been no great depression, presumably these would have grown slowly in response to state requests for financial help. But the depression created welfare problems far beyond the financial capacity of the states. As a temporary measure the central government undertook support for the unemployed; but as a permanent measure the United States guided the states in forming unemployment insurance programs. Once it had accepted these welfare responsibilities it also seemed reasonable to support a general Old Age and Survivors' insurance program that, because of the mobility of Americans, could hardly be run by any government other than the federal one.

Recreation and Culture. Despite a persistent myth about the materialism of American life and the cultural indifference of its governments, the fact is that Americans have for a long time pursued culture with an avidity unparalleled in any other society. Governments have participated in this pursuit in appropriate ways, not all of which, of course, have suited the most refined taste of the period. I suppose it is the failure to suit the most refined taste that has led many to overlook the support governments have given to the arts. But the support has existed at all levels from the early part of the 19th century onward and deserves mention. Because of the size of the country and the complexity of our governmental structure and because of our long-standing effort to educate everybody, we have required an extraordinarily large number of public buildings, the competitions for which have done much to encourage architecture. The tradition has suggested that buildings and parks be adorned with paintings and statuary, which has meant a basic subsidy of these arts. Furthermore, almost every metropolitan center with a population of 100,000 or more has art museums, some private, but many public. As for letters, the federal government during the 19th century subsidized some men of letters with political sinecures (though perhaps not as many as elsewhere in the world); but the great subsidy for letters is the free public library movement that spread throughout state and local governments in the late 19th century and thereby both subsidized authors and made their products available to the whole society. Next to letters, music has been the most heavily subsidized of the arts, from town bands (an almost universal feature of 19th-century and even 20th-century state subsidy) to symphony orchestras. Music has been incorporated generally into the secondary school curriculum, a major subsidy absent from most other nations. Of the performing and decorative arts, the only one not supported in depth by the several governments is the theater, yet even in this there is indirect support through the provision of buildings for performances. Typically, the support of the arts has come mostly from states or their subsidiaries rather than from the central government, although it too has participated where appropriate and the short-lived WPA program for unemployed artists during the 1930's subsidized decorative arts, letters, and even the performing arts.

The preponderance of the states is just about as great in the field of recreation, although here the federal government makes notable and expensive contributions. Cities began the development of their park systems in the mid-19th century and these today have become one of the most attractive features of American urbanism, distinguishing it rather sharply from European and Asiatic urbanism, which lack extensive park resources. In the 20th century, cities have established systematic recreation programs in their parks and playgrounds, supplementing these with zoos and gardens. But the federal government also has created parks. As a consequence of the conservation movement at the turn of the century vast wilderness areas (especially in the West) were set aside as national parks. On a lesser scale the state governments have followed a policy of preserving areas of special interest so that there is now also a large state park program. In short, both levels of government have extensive park resources. In area, the national system is probably greater; but measured by expenditure the state and local system probably surpasses the federal.

Public Health. Owing to the explosion of medical knowledge in the last century, public health has become a concern of all levels of government. Even before the explosion began, the provision of sewers (previously discussed as a utility) and asylums (previously discussed as an aid to the handicapped) was recognized as a public health function. But with the development of epidemiology, public health became a major political concern. Initially local and state governments undertook to report on deaths and to regulate the response to epidemics, *e.g.*, vaccination and isolation. Later, as the facts of disease-transmission were recognized, pure food and drug statutes were passed by most governments, including the federal. Since national markets existed for most foods and drugs, federal supervision of these matters largely superseded state supervision. As industrial diseases and hazards were recognized, safety programs were established to deal with them; and since most of the industries were national (*e.g.*, mining), so were the safety and health programs. As drug manufacturing came to be recognized as a major health factor, inspection and supervision programs were established, chiefly under federal aegis, since the drug market, too, is national in nature.

The present state of the division of labor in this area is hard to assess. Every locality has its public health officers; but the crucial programs seem to be in the hands of the national government. A paradigm: Two generations ago the control and therapy of tuberculosis was entirely in state control; a generation ago the control and therapy of syphilis was in joint state and federal hands; today the research on cancer, heart disease, and mental health is largely under federal auspices. The point is that the direction of medical energy on the main attackable diseases has gradually shifted from state to nation. To some degree the nature of diseases has been basic to the shifting; but even more basic has been the availability of financial support.

It would be difficult to say which level, state or national, now predominates in the field of public health. Perhaps the appropriate generalization is that, with some exceptions in each case, states and localities do most of the routine work, whereas the nation does most of the work on the frontiers of public health. Financially, state and local expenditures are probably greater.

New knowledge. Most governmental support for the acquisition of new knowledge comes under the rubric of economic development, but some patronage of pure research, of finding things out for the sake of finding them out, has always been undertaken by civilized governments. The system of patents, which is meant to encourage full disclosure, probably benefits economic development primarily, but the system of copyrights seems purely to encourage and reward the arts and sciences. These are, of course, federal by reason of the Constitution; but other patronage might conceivably come from either level, presumably from the more affluent level. Since the federal government has usually been the more affluent, it is the one that has supported the most pure research. It has sponsored scientific societies, supported exploration of remote places (not only on this continent but also at the poles), and in the period since World War II has directly supported a large amount of research in both physical and biological sciences that could at the moment have very little practical application. So far as I know, states have never done anything like this directly, though of course they do much indirectly by supporting universities.

VII CENTRALIZED FEDERALISM IN THE UNITED STATES

This chapter contains an examination in nineteen categories of action of the degree of centralization (or peripheralization) of federalism in the United States. It is apparent that one theme running through these brief verbal descriptions is that the federal government has acquired more duties, in relation to the states, over the years. Both kinds of governments have grown with the nation, but the federal government seems to have become somewhat more conspicuous than that of the states.

This conclusion is summarized numerically in Table 3.3, which indicates, for each of the seventeen substantive areas of spending money, the relative position of federal and constituent governments at four time periods. The entries are defined thus:

1 The functions are performed exclusively or almost exclusively by the federal government.
2 The functions are performed predominantly by the federal government, although the state governments play a significant secondary role.
3 The functions are performed by federal and state governments in about equal proportions.
4 The functions are performed predominantly by the state governments, although the federal government plays a significant secondary role.
5 The functions are performed exclusively or almost exclusively by the state governments.
– The functions were not recognized to exist at the time.

The choice of a particular entry is, of course, my highly subjective judgment based only on my immersion in the study. Others might disagree with my assignments, but by keeping the discriminations crude, that is, by using only a five-point scale, disagreements are probably minimized. The last row of the table shows the average for each of the time points of all functions then recognized to exist. Since the seventeen (or fourteen, or fifteen) categories of functions are by no means of equal significance politically or socially, it may well be argued that the average is without meaning. Therefore, I have made the same kind of judgment for possibly equally significant groups of functions (external affairs, internal order, trade, and welfare) and the result is approximately the same.

But granted that the federal government has become administratively somewhat more conspicuous than the states, the question remains: Does this table of American experience support the administrative theory of federalism? I think not. Under this theory, administrative centralization is what is supposed to preserve and maintain the central government. But if one looks at the

Table 3.3 THE DEGREE OF CENTRALIZATION IN THE UNITED STATES BY SUBSTANTIVE FUNCTIONS AND AT POINTS IN TIME

	Functions	*ca. 1790*	*ca. 1850*	*ca. 1910*	*ca. 1964*
1	External affairs	4	1	1	1
2	Public safety	5	4	4	4
3	Property rights	5	5	4	4
4	Civic rights	5	5	5	3
5	Morality	5	5	5	5
6	Patriotism	3	3	3	3
7	Money and credit	3	4	3	1
8	Transport and communication	4	4	2	2
9	Utilities	5	5	5	4
10	Production and distribution	5	5	4	2
11	Economic development	3	4	3	2
12	Resources	—	—	2	2
13	Education	—	5	5	4
14	Indigency	5	5	5	2
15	Recreation	—	4	4	3
16	Health	—	—	4	3
17	Knowledge	1	1	1	2
	Average	4.1	4.0	3.5	2.8

crucial period for the survival of federalism in the United States; that is, from 1790 to 1850, it appears that some functions were centralized and others were decentralized. Military centralization was matched by economic decentralization (cf. rows 1, 7, and 11). We have no easy way of knowing whether or not these reallocations were in areas of comparable importance; but we do know that the reallocations were not all in the same direction — as they have been since the Civil War. And since they are not all in the same direction we cannot affirm that administrative centralization is what preserved the federal bargain in the pre-Civil War era.

On the other hand, the sharing of administration is what is supposed to preserve the guarantees to the states. Yet, according to the table, sharing has declined notably in the last period (*i.e.*, from 1910 to the present) whereas the fundamental guarantees to the states seem as strong as ever. I conclude, therefore, that the administrative theory is totally inadequate to explain the maintenance of federalism. Unfortunately, most American students of the subject have been deeply attracted to the theory; hence it has tended to obscure constitutional realities. I will be content if this essay has no other impact but to disabuse scholars of their faith in the clearly false administrative theory of federalism.

4

Institutions of federalism in the United States

In the previous chapter, the possibility was considered that one condition for keeping the bargain of federalism was the gradual centralization and sharing of governmental functions. This is an initially attractive hypothesis because it seems to fit with contemporary experience in the United States. Yet the history summarized and categorized systematically in the previous chapter does not bear out the administrative theory of federalism. So we must start over again in our hunt for an explanation.

Of course, a sufficient condition for the maintenance of federalism is the long continuance of precisely those circumstances which called forth the bargain in the first place as, *e.g.*, Switzerland until 1848. But this is not the kind of explanation we are after here, for we want to know what conditions help to keep the bargain after the original conditions disappear.

In Chapter 1, I suggested that the distinction between centralized and peripheralized federalisms lay in the ability of the rulers of the central and constituent governments to overawe each other.

In centralized federalisms, the ability of the center to overawe the constituents is thus clearly a condition of keeping the bargain, so long as it does not proceed as far as complete unification. Likewise, in peripheralized federalisms, the lack of the ability to overawe is a condition of breaking the bargain. The examination of this distinction suggests that the conditions of keeping the federal bargain may be found here.

Let us arrange the ability of one kind of government or the other to overawe according to this scale

A The central government can completely overawe the constituent governments.
B The central government cannot completely overawe the constituents, but it can keep them from overruling its own decisions.
C The constituent governments cannot completely overawe the rulers of the center, but they can significantly vary the behavior of officials of the center, though central officials cannot overawe them.
D The constituent governments can unilaterally completely overawe the rulers of the center.

Manifestly, if either situations A or D exist then the federal bargain cannot be maintained. If A exists, then the bargain can be broken by depriving the constituent governments of all independence of action. If D exists, then the bargain can be broken by so depriving the center. Hence, neither can be conditions for keeping the bargain. On the other hand, if situations B or C exist, either is sufficient to maintain the bargain. If B exists, then the center can guarantee its own independence and may not take it away from the constituent units. If C exists, the constituents can guarantee their own independence and may not take it from the center. Either B or C is thus a sufficient condition for keeping the bargain. Condition B is centralized federalism and condition C is peripheralized federalism.

In short, the sum and spirit of the political institutions provide for the keeping or the breaking of the bargain. If the sum and spirit of the institutions are such that they can be summarized by either sentence B or C, then the bargain may be kept. Otherwise, it may not. What I propose to do in this chapter, then, is to examine the main federal institutions in the United States to show that they can be said in sum to possess the spirit of sentence B. In the following chapter the institutions of some of the older federalisms will be reviewed in order to classify them as instances of A, B, or C. (Obviously, none can be D, for then they would not be old. They can be A, however, by becoming substantially unitary while maintaining the trappings of a bygone federalism.)

Specifically in Chapter 3, I shall examine both consciously constructed institutions (*e.g.*, those planned in the Constitution, whether they worked out as planned or not) and institutions that the framers unconsciously assumed to be constants (*e.g.*, the electoral system) in order to discover their effects on federalism. I shall arrange these examinations in order of my estimate of the importance of the institution in bringing about the present form of federalism in the United States. The four main institutions considered are:

(1) the United States Senate, which the framers intended as a peripheralizing institution, but which has in fact never had this effect:

(2) the system of political parties, which the framers treated as an immutable given and which they did not discuss, but which has turned out to be the main peripheralizing influence in the system:

(3) the federal executive and judiciary, which the framers planned as centralizing institutions and which in fact have had this effect; and

(4) the directions and degrees of patriotism, which also the framers assumed to be an immutable constant, but which has changed greatly over the years with significant effects on federalism.

I THE UNITED STATES SENATE

In the United States one main peripheralizing institution is, purportedly, the Senate, at least in original intent. The fact that the Senate never served this purpose is one reason why the United States has always been a bit on the centralized side of the scale.

In the Philadelphia Convention of 1787, the compromise between the large and small states that produced the Senate was intended to carry forward into the new government the same kind of participation in lawmaking that state governments had under the Articles. In the Congress of the Articles, the state governments controlled the legislative behavior of their representatives so that laws were actually approved, not at Philadelphia where the Congress sat, but at each of the state capitols. The notion of representing the state governments in the Senate, especially since the stated reason for this representation was to prevent legislative tyranny by the large states over the small, thus constitutes an attempt to preserve in the Constitution the peripheralization of the Articles. I think there can be little doubt that most of the framers thought they had done just this, that they had modified it and made it more workable, but had nevertheless preserved it. But in fact they had not. What they had instead done was to inject a peripheralizing feature into what was essentially a new and centralized scheme. Not surprisingly, the centralized tone of the basic system affected the operation of the Senate so that it was never able to operate as a peripheralizer. Some of our centralization may thus be said to be a result of the framers' oversight.

The Congressmen of the Articles were creatures of the state legislatures, but the Senators under the Constitution have always been independent. The Seventeenth Amendment finally recognized this fact by changing the Senatorial electors from the state legislators to the people of the states.[1] What made the Congressmen of the Articles the mere creatures of state legislatures was the fact that state legislatures (1) elected the Congressmen, (2) regularly instructed them how to vote and (3) could and did recall them at any time. The framers of the Constitution, possibly believing that item (1) was sufficient to guarantee the dependence of Senators on state legislatures, did not carry items (2) and (3) over into the Constitution. By failing to do so they rendered

[1] This and several subsequent paragraphs are based on William H. Riker, "The Senate and American Federalism," *American Political Science Review*, Vol. 49 (1955) pp. 452-69.

state legislative control quite tenuous and ultimately non-existent.

We have no way of knowing whether or not the omission of items (2) or (3) was accidental or deliberate. But we do know that in the first Congress, the House, by a large majority, refused to add the right to instruct to the First Amendment. (The matter was to some degree a partisan issue, with federalists opposing instructions and proto-republicans favoring them; and this was, with some variation, the party division on the subject for the next 40 years.) As for recall, the framers may have intended the provision that each house be judge of its membership as a device to prevent recall (which it most effectively does); but they may have had no more in mind than the settlement of contested elections. Again the fixed term of six years may have been intended to prevent recall; but it seems more likely that it was simply part of a larger pattern of centralized government and had no specific institutional intent. We do know, however, that proposed constitutional amendments providing for recall of Senators were defeated in the Senate in the early years of the Republic. So, even if the omissions were accidental to begin with or just a part of the larger pattern of centralization, the officials of the national government soon made them deliberate protections of Senators from their immediate constituents, the state legislators.

Without the power to recall Senators, state legislatures' instructions were not particularly effective. State legislatures continued to instruct Senators right up to the passage of the Seventeenth Amendment according to the traditional formula "Be it resolved that our Senators in Congress are hereby instructed, and our Representatives are requested, to vote for . . . ." But instructions were obeyed when palatable and disobeyed when not. Certainly the threat of the next election was not sufficient to induce obedience. If instructions were unpalatable and the next election was several years away, then Senators could and did ignore them in the hope that a different partisan majority would exist in the state legislature when the next Senatorial election occurred. If instructions were unpalatable and the next election was soon to come then Senators could ignore them in the certain knowledge that they would not be re-elected anyway no matter how servile their behavior.

Those who held to a peripheralized version of the Union searched for some sanction to enforce instructions throughout the first half-century of the Republic and they found a partial substitute for recall in the notion of forced resignations. This notion consisted of the doctrine that, if faced with instructions that he could not conscientiously obey, a Senator should, as a matter of personal honor, resign so that the state legislature could elect a new Senator who could conscientiously obey. This doctrine became popular, especially in the South, in the Jacksonian period and Jackson used his friends in state legislatures to force the resignation of his enemies in the Senate. But Jackson's use of the device also probably destroyed it. Since it was intended only to insert the states into the national decision process, it was clearly misused when one set of national officials used it to fight another set. Not surprisingly, men were disillusioned with it and even Southern Senators gradually found that it did not hurt their personal honor at all to vote contrary to instructions and to keep their seats. When this alternative to recall failed, no other was found, so that by the 1840's Senators were completely emancipated from day-to-day dependence on their constituents, the state legislators.

The sanction of re-election, though weak, remained; but even it ceased to have meaning by the end of the 19th century. In the early years of the Republic, candidates for the Senate did not start their campaigns (or, often, even announce their candidacy) until after the members of the state legislature were elected. The Senators' constituents were the legislators, not the people at large; so it was felt proper to wait until constituents had been created before soliciting their votes. Sporadically through the first century, especially when ideological contests were most intense, announced candidates for the Senate campaigned for candidates for the state legislature who were pledged to support them. (The famous Lincoln–Douglas debates occurred during one such campaign, one of the first in which legislative candidates were systematically pledged to the Senatorial candidates.) This kind of campaigning fundamentally changed the relationship between the legislature and the Senator. Without the Senatorial campaign, the candidate for the Senate really did have to solicit support from the state legislators, making promises often about his future behavior. The legislature was thus the master, at least for the brief time of the election. With the Senatorial campaign, however, all this changed. It was the state legislator who owed his office to the popular appeal of the Senatorial candidate to whom he was pledged. By the end of the 19th century, Senatorial campaigns had become almost universal west of the Appalachians, thereby emancipating most Senators from their dependence on the state officials and severing whatever channel still remained to carry national decisions back to the states. The Seventeenth Amendment simply formalized the severance that had already occurred.

II PARTY ORGANIZATION

As nearly all observers have pointed out, political parties are highly decentralized in the United States. They lack unity on a national level with respect to both platforms and leaders. City and county (and, rarely, state) organizations are the bodies that control most nominations for Congress and for state and local offices. Even the nominations to the Presidency are often controlled by confederations of local party and state leaders, rather than by clearly national leaders.

The consequence is, not that states control national decisions — it would take more than local control of nominations to bring about that effect — but that the nation cannot control state decisions. The result is a standoff, which is what, I suppose, is intended in the federal bargain.

The historic localism of our parties is reflected in and probably reinforced by two important constitutional provisions: (1) the requirement that Representatives be residents of the state from which elected and (2) the permission to state legislatures to prescribe the manner of elections. The first provision was probably intended to prevent what progressive opinion of the day regarded as an abuse in the English system. Then as now in Britain the Members of Parliament seldom were residents of their constituencies, although then, when many constituencies were rotten boroughs, the lack of residence seemed closely associated with a fundamental distortion of representative government. What the framers therefore required was probably meant as no more than an indirect provision against the abuse of rotten boroughs, but it has operated to require that representation be local and to reinforce the assumption that control of nominations is vested in local party organizations. The second provision, the permission given to state legislatures to govern elections in the absence of national legislation, was intended to reassure the states that they were not being deprived by the Constitution of control of the basic representative process. Hence it was consciously peripheralizing in its intent and doubtless also in its effect.

But these two provisions in the formal written Constitution are merely minor reflections of the style and spirit of the deeper unwritten Constitution. In this Constitution, as I understand it, one universal rule is that decisions are to be made at the lowest level (*i.e.*, by the smallest units) consonant with efficient operation. This rule appears in religious life, with the historic dominance in the United States of non-hierarchical churches; it appears in economic life, with our fairly intense preference for competitive markets of small-scale entrepreneurs; it appears in political life, with the proliferation of special-interest groups. With respect to party organization it means, of course, that if no great harm is done to governmental operation, party organization is to be primarily local in nature.

This localism has been supported by two conditions, one of which is simply tradition and the other the absence of any effective device for unifying party ideologies and organization. About tradition one need say little, except that the force of tradition exists and, given an initial localism, tradition of course perpetuates it. About the absence of any effective device for unification, one needs to say quite a bit to indicate how seriously national leaders have sought for one without, however, conspicuous success.

To examine the absence of a device for unification, consider the operation of the office of the President: first, electorally, the nomination of a candidate for President and then the election of a President, the two electoral processes usually regarded as the most important ones in our political system. At least when the sitting President is not a candidate for renomination in a convention, the process of winning a nomination is a process of forming (over a period of one to two years) a coalition large enough to win. The several prospective candidates naturally have to reward the delegates who enter their several coalitions. Some delegates, especially those who are chosen in primaries, may be rewarded cheaply (*i.e.*, with promises about ideology). But others must be rewarded in more expensive ways, *e.g.*, with promises of high office for their leaders, with promises of specific policy decisions, with promises of help in local elections, etc. In this coalition-building process, the prospective candidates typically devote full time for about two years to bargaining and bargaining and bargaining. If one regards the election campaign as a process of candidates offering bargains to marginal voters, then the bargaining continues right up to the election — and soon after the election is over the bargaining starts again for the next one.

Or consider the President's relationship with Congress: If parties were nationally oriented, then the President would be able to count on substantially complete support from his partisans in Congress. But one of the most well-known facts about our system is that he cannot. Instead, to put any measure through he must bargain, even with his own partisans, whom, in the classic (but false) theory of parties, he has already bought with the cheap currency of ideology.

In short, the life of a President, who is the main national official, is one of constant bargaining — to get the votes to get nominated, to get the votes to get elected, to get the votes to get bills through Congress, to get the votes to get renominated, etc., etc.

This constant bargaining is expensive: Time consumed in making one bargain is consumed forever and cannot be used to make another. And this fact is a significant limitation on what a President can accomplish. Not surprisingly, therefore, most Presidents have tried to invent an ideology which they could persuade their partisans to accept and which, once accepted, would serve as a sufficient reward for votes tendered. Such an ideology would take the place of bargaining and permit its creator to minimize the costs of bargaining itself and thus to accomplish greater numbers of things.

The significant feature of Presidential attempts to substitute ideological commitment for bargaining is that it has usually failed, or at least has not succeeded for very long. Rarely has a President been able to leave it to a successor. Sometimes the effort of creating an ideology takes so much time that its creator is nearly out of office by the time the ideology is beginning to work.

The Presidents who worked hardest and most effectively to create an ideology were: Jefferson, Jackson, Lincoln, Theodore Roosevelt, and Franklin Roosevelt. Let us consider their experience.

Jefferson emerged as the focal point for the anti-federalist feelings as early as 1791. For the next ten years he spent a major portion of his time trying to organize these emotions into a base for party organization and a reasonably coherent ideology. As President he continued the process for the whole of his eight years in office and indeed, even after he left office, he continued to play the elder-statesman role in the Republican party until his very old age. He succeeded to a certain degree, perhaps more than any of his heirs. He did create an ideology and organization that wiped the Federalist party out. He did create an ideology that reduced his load of bargaining during his first few years of office. But despite this success, his ideology and organization was of little help in the problems of his second term (*i.e.*, the policy of the embargo) which he had to solve in the bargaining way, and he left to his immediate successors a party organization so torn apart and an ideology so tarnished that they were forced to operate exclusively by the method of bargaining.

Jackson, who came to office at a time when national parties had almost ceased to exist, is chiefly memorable for his re-creation of national parties, an achievement that was entirely incidental to his struggle to create an ideology for the manipulation of voters and legislators. He became a candidate in 1823 and he became a serious ideologist when he lost by the so-called corrupt bargain of 1825 — the kind of bargain, incidentally, which all non-ideological candidates must make. In the next twelve years he fashioned an ideology and an organization around himself as a leader, one of the few reasonably enduring structures in our political history. But it took him most of the twelve years to create it so that he himself had relatively little opportunity to use it. His great effort was the battle to destroy the United States Bank, which he began in 1830 and which he concluded only in 1836, after numerous setbacks in the intervening years. And even then the conclusion was inconclusive, for he had not the time to build an alternative organization. He did leave, however, a good organization and a viable ideology to his two hand-picked successors, Van Buren and Polk. Van Buren accomplished little, because his partisans soon lost control of Congress. But Polk, though no creator of ideology, was an expert manipulator, who carried through most of the Jacksonian program. Expert bargainer that Polk was, however, it would be difficult to imagine him carrying through the program without the minimization of bargaining costs that the Jacksonian ideology permitted.

Lincoln had less time to create an ideology than either of the previously discussed Presidents. Not surprisingly, therefore, his ideology lasted a shorter time and was less transmissible to other leaders. Entering the campaign for national office only two years before he was elected (as a minority choice), he was forced to develop his ideology of Unionism during the four years he was in office. Although the ideology remains as a part of the national heritage, it was of no use to his immediate successors, one of whom failed miserably as a President because he tried to use it and others of whom preferred to distort it (and thereby weakened it as a cost-cutting device).

Theodore Roosevelt was engaged in creating an ideology most of his adult life, but the ideology he created did not attract much national attention until the day he assumed office, quite accidentally. Hence he had only the seven years of his Presidency to try to impose this ideology on the party he led. He was not generally successful. True, he was enabled to pick his successor, something no President since Jackson had been able to do; and also he was able to reorganize the Republican party in several states, especially his own state of New York, to accept and be guided by his ideology. Nevertheless he was not able to use his ideology to minimize bargaining costs, for he always faced quite implacable conservatives in the Republican leadership in Congress. And when his chosen successor turned out not to be a puppet, TR's ideology also turned out to be insufficient to beat him either in convention or in election.

Franklin Roosevelt had probably better opportunities to impose an ideology on his party than any of the Presidents previously discussed. Though he came to office relatively unknown — as compared with Jefferson and Jackson — he held office for over twelve years and thus had a longer hold on the main forum for creating an ideology than any other man. It is perhaps too soon to assess the significance for subsequent Presidents of the ideology they inherited from him; but for FDR himself one can point out that though the ideology undoubtedly facilitated his unprecedented re-elections, it never reduced his need to bargain with Congressmen. Indeed, when his ideological and organizational success were presumably at their height (in 1937 and 1941) his necessity to bargain with Congressmen was also greatest. Significantly, the ideology he left to Truman never worked for domestic legislation, for which it was fashioned, though it did work in conjunction with Truman's consummate bargaining skill in the area of foreign affairs.

The Presidents mentioned are commonly regarded as more effective than most others and probably the reason they have been more effective is that they have bound voters and Congressmen to themselves with an ideological tie that eliminates, to some degree, the high costs of bargaining. But as the survey indicates, no President has been able to create an ideology sufficiently powerful to eliminate bargaining and only Jackson created an ideology that worked as well for his successors as for himself. This relative failure, which I believe is rooted in the decentralized character of the party system, indicates that localism is a powerful agent in maintaining the guarantee to the states in the federal bargain.

What some Presidents have tried to do with ideology, nearly all Presidents have tried by manipulating the organization of their parties. The crucial kind of activity here is the attempt to control the composition of Congress. If a Congressman owes his seat to the agency of the President, presumably then he is willing to do what the President asks without much hesitation, thereby also eliminating the President's cost of bargaining. Most Presidents, at least for the last century or so, have campaigned for their partisans for Congress with greater or lesser degrees of enthusiasm. But, given the ideological spread in our parties, given their lack of cohesion in legislative behavior, the election of partisans is not enough.

So most Presidents also have tried to control the composition of their parties by controlling nominations, especially for Congress, but also for state offices such as governorships and party offices such as state chairmanships. Most such attempts are probably made in conversation, often as part of discussions on the allocation of patronage. Hence their frequency and force are difficult for the scholar to assess. It seems likely that in the latter part of the 19th century, when the President could dispense large amounts of really valuable patronage, Presidential control of nominations was greater than it now is. But this is a guess for which I know no possible technique of verification. One feature of Presidential attempts to control nominations is necessarily semi-public, however, and hence is something the scholar can assess. This is the attempt to influence the selection of nominees in state party primaries. To influence, the President must ask voters to support a candidate for the nomination and this is necessarily a public act. One way to look at Presidential attempts to control the composition of their parties is, then, to study these semi-public acts.

Since Senatorial nominations were forced into public primaries only in this century, most widely since 1913, the obvious beginning point for such a survey is 1914. William Bast and I have checked the *Index* of *The New York Times* from 1914 through 1957 for all instances of any sort of Presidential enunciation of a preference for a candidate in a Congressional primary of the President's own party.[2] Altogether we found 38 instances of such public announcements, eight of which occurred in 1918 and eleven in 1938. Of the seven Presidents involved, Roosevelt was the most active, accounting for fifteen instances. Wilson and

[2] For a report of this investigation, see William Bast, *Presidential Participation in Congressional Primary Elections of His Own Party* (Appleton, Wis.: Lawrence College Library, typewritten, 1958).

Truman come next, accounting for ten and nine instances respectively, whereas Harding, Coolidge, Hoover, and Eisenhower accounted for one each. On a per-year-in-office basis, Truman was the most active (1.29 instance per year); Eisenhower was the least active. But the two really memorable clusters of instances were Wilson's effort to eliminate anti-war Democrats in 1918 and Roosevelt's effort to eliminate anti-New Deal Democrats in 1938.

Of course, the most obviously outstanding feature of this survey is the paucity of instances. Presidents seem to have been quite reluctant to speak out publicly in Congressional primaries and the reasons may be evident from an examination of the two clusters of instances.

In the spring of 1918, Wilson began a campaign to elect a "War Congress," one that would support his management of the war in a more enthusiastic manner. His plan included campaign support for the Congressional supporters, in both parties, of his war program. (Since the definition of support for his program was, of course, up to Wilson, only rarely did a Republican qualify.) But before the campaign, he proposed to weed out of the Southern Democratic party some of those who helped him least. Not all his uncooperative partisans had opponents, or opponents who could be expected to behave differently on war issues. But for some of those who did, Wilson supported the opponent in the primary. He did so, usually, in response to an obviously inspired request from some prominent local leader for Wilson's opinion of the incumbent. On receipt of the request, Wilson then wrote a reply, either denouncing the incumbent or actually endorsing the incumbent's opponent. These interchanges were, of course, carefully arranged. Wilson in effect chose those incumbents who were likely to lose and supported their opponents at least inferentially. And in some few instances he may actually have negotiated with local leaders about who the opponents were to be. On the whole, Wilson was successful, for his men won in four Southern primaries and lost in a fifth. The relative success of Wilson's purge, which was the first such ever attempted publicly, was obscured, however, by the fact that Republicans gained control of Congress at the general election.

Roosevelt attempted a similar purge twenty years later, although in this instance the aims were strictly partisan. He started his campaign trip with a fireside chat, asserting:[3]

> As head of the Democratic party . . . charged with carrying out the definitely liberal declaration of principles set forth in the 1936 Democratic platform, I feel I have every right to speak in those few instances where there may be a clear issue between the candidates for a Democratic nomination involving those principles or involving a clear misuse of my own name.

This explanation seems to suggest a deep reluctance on the President's part and, indeed, most historians are agreed that the initiative in the purge came from Roosevelt's "kitchen cabinet" rather than himself. Nevertheless, he seemed to feel also that his inability to bargain successfully with, especially, Southern Democrats forced him to try this expedient. Owing to his apparent vacillation, however, Roosevelt was ill-prepared: he started late in the season, later than Wilson, and he failed to consult with local leaders. As a result, his endorsed candidates did poorly: when he endorsed incumbents, they won except in one instance; when he endorsed the opponents of incumbents, they lost, except in one Congressional district in New York City. Notably, the two main antagonists, Senators George of Georgia and Tydings of Maryland, triumphantly survived Roosevelt's endorsements of their rather second-rate opponents, both of whom had come forward long before Roosevelt began his campaign. In short, the so-called purge of 1938 was popularly regarded as a failure, as in fact it was from the point of view of both organizational control and popular estimation.[4]

As I noted previously, the most obviously significant feature of Presidential attempts to influence the outcomes of Congressional primaries in their own parties is the paucity of instances. One reason for the paucity is immediately apparent from the foregoing examination of the two clusters of instances: these clusters have concerned Democratic Presidents and Southern Democratic Con-

[3] *The Public Papers and Addresses of Franklin D. Roosevelt, 1938* (New York: Macmillan, 1941), Vol. 7, p. 399.

[4] For a detailed account of this purge, see William H. Riker, *Democracy in the United States* (New York: Macmillan, 1953) pp. 285-93.

gressmen; that is, Congressmen from substantially one-party districts, and this fact suggests that Presidents have been willing to undertake systematic purges only when there is no danger of contributing to the final victory of the other party. There is good *a priori* reason for such caution: Suppose the parties in a state are approximately of equal strength. Suppose also that the President by his intervention in a Congressional primary to support one faction in his party drives the other faction into either a neutral position in the general election or even a positive preference for the candidate of the other party. Then his attempt to reduce the costs of bargaining by organizational control simply results in an increase in the cost of bargaining because in the general election the candidate of the other party wins. In such circumstances, elementary political caution suggests that the President avoid potentially self-defeating attempts to control the organization of his party. Most Presidents have in fact been cautious in just this way — witness not only the paucity of instances but also the reluctance apparent in Roosevelt's initial statement at the beginning of the 1938 purge. Hence, I conclude that the chief constraint on Presidential or national control of party organization is the existence of the two-party system.

It is commonly said that the two-party system enforces a kind of ideological conformity on the political system, by forcing parties to present substantially similar candidates. But if, as I have just shown, it allows for organizational decentralization and hence ideological diversity, one wonders how it can simultaneously induce conformity. Actually, however, the two statements are not in conflict. The conformity is induced by the matching of pairs of candidates in elections and exists in each geographic district in which an election is held. (An important special case is the election of the President, in which the district is, effectively if not legally, the whole nation — and it is the operation of the two-party system in this case that usually leads to the assertion that it induces conformity.) But there is nothing in the system to guarantee that all the Democratic members of the electoral pairs will be like each other more than like Republicans. Indeed, so long as the two-party system operates within a decentralized context, the probability is that Republicans and Democrats who face each other in an election will be more alike than either all Democrats or all Republicans. Thus the two-party system induces similarity between parties by districts, but encourages (by perpetuating decentralization) dissimilarity within parties.

So, I conclude, the decentralization of the two-party system is sufficient to prevent national leaders (*e.g.*, Presidents) from controlling their partisans by either organizational or ideological devices. As such, this decentralized party system is the main protector of the integrity of states in our federalism.

III PRESIDENT AND COURT

The framers undoubtedly intended the Presidency to be the main centralizing institution, as in fact it has been. They took great pains to devise a method of electing the President that would guarantee his independence from state governments (as well as the national legislature). And though the electoral method they devised has not worked as they intended — they expected a kinglike figure, a Washington, to emerge from the quadrennial elections and indeed they fashioned the Presidency with Washington in mind — still it has given the President a national constituency and has thereby removed him from dependence on state officials. If it has not always produced Presidents like Washington, it may be that this is less the fault of the device than of the limited supply of national heroes.

Having rendered the President largely independent of state governments, the framers gave him all the powers that the British Crown then possessed, although they slightly limited some of them. Thus they guaranteed the continued viability of the central government. The most important power was, of course, the military–diplomatic one, which, as I described in the previous chapter, became especially important after 1815. Had this nation turned out to be one in which force was continually needed to maintain the Union (as, *e.g.*, Mexico), then very probably a much greater degree of centralization would have occurred sooner than it did. The fact that we have had only one Civil War, desperate as it was, has blinded us to the fact that the main events in a centralizing process are the military subjugation of would-be peripheralizers. In this sense Lincoln is the great centralizer, for he pushed the facilities of his office as far as was needed to stop attempted peripheralization and indeed to centralize the whole process of government.

And in this century the administrative centralization, though partially occasioned by economic necessity, has usually been preceded and accompanied by exploitation of the President's military and diplomatic authority. Theodore Roosevelt, Wilson, Franklin Roosevelt, and Truman all used their military powers creatively and aggressively, often to accomplish what they could not accomplish by other means. All this is a story often told, however, so I see no need to repeat it here.[5]

Aside from the Presidency, the other main centralizing institution is the Supreme Court. Many writers on federalism, especially those with a background in law, interpret the Court as the "arbiter of federalism"; *i.e.*, the agency that decides on the pace and extent of centralization, and assert that the Court, by its gradual changing of the boundaries between the work of the states and the work of the nation, has been a major force for centralization. This interpretation is on its face fallacious and could only come from an overspecialized view of the political process. The Court is an organization without much political or military force and therefore cannot be expected to occasion or even to pace constitutional change. A more accurate way to interpret the role of the Court, which is by construction and its framers' probable intent admittedly a wholly centralized institution, is to say that the Court hastens the process of centralization when it is in phase with the ideology of the Presidency and cannot impede centralization when it is not.

The Court is dependent on the Presidency for its renewal, but since the judges have life tenure, it is quite possible that at any particular time the ideological tone of the two institutions may be quite different. Four cases can be distinguished:

1. The President and the Court are striving for greater centralization.

[5] See, for example, William H. Riker, *Democracy in the United States*, Chapter 6.

2. The President and the Court are content to maintain the status quo.
3. The President is striving to centralize and the Court to maintain the status quo.
4. The President is content to maintain the status quo and the Court to centralize.

Examples of case 1 are the periods 1938-53 (Roosevelt and Truman) and 1790-95 (Washington); examples of case 2 are 1835-60 (the Taney Court) and 1869-1933 (the Republican dominance); examples of case 3 are 1861–65 (Civil War), 1933-37 (New Deal); and the only clear example of case 4 is to be found sporadically during the period 1801-34 (the Marshall Court).

The crucial question is about cases 3 and 4. Can the Court resist the President's attempts to centralize and can the Court centralize when Presidents are not eager to do so? A brief look at the examples demonstrates that the answer to both questions is negative. The Taney Court was powerless to inhibit Lincoln's military centralization and the Hughes Court was able to resist Roosevelt's centralization only for about two years. On the other hand, though Marshall made many bold pronouncements, the centralization that occurred in his era was mostly military, with which he had nothing to do. Economic centralization, in which he was interested, actually declined during his period on the bench. It seems clear, therefore, that the Court has significance for federalism only when it is the handmaiden of the political branches, especially the Presidential branch. And as a handmaiden, it is of only secondary importance for our analysis.

IV THE SPIRIT OF AMERICAN FEDERALISM

This survey indicates, I believe, that our federalism qualifies as an instance of category B (in which "the central government cannot completely overawe the constituents, but it can keep them from overruling its own decisions"). The independent institutions of the central government are strong, especially militarily, and over the years they have grown stronger. Probably the federal executive and legislative are more influential in the society as a whole than the sum of the states together. Since the states have never acted as a unit against the center, we do not know for certain whether or not this assertion is true. But a weaker assertion, that the center is more influential than a coalition of as many as half the states, is almost certainly true. Furthermore this strength is based on a direct relationship with the electorate, without the intervention of the state governments. This relationship, not originally intended, has come about through the modification of the Senate and a similar modification of the electoral college.

But, for all the strength of the central institutions, the state governments are independent of them also, for they too have a direct relationship with the electorate. The institution that seems to be most significant in separating the relationship between center and electorate, on the one hand, and states and electorate, on the other hand, seems to be a widely decentralized party system.

Thus the conditions of category B are fulfilled: the central government is strong and independent, but the states are to some degree independent too.

Standing behind these specific institutional arrangements is a yet more fundamental feature of our life, which is the sense of national and state identification. It is very likely that the basic condition that allows for both centralization and resistance to centralization is the degree of popular identification with national and state governments. If citizens, when asked their citizen-identification, reply "I am an American" to the exclusion of "I am a Hoosier" or "I am a Texan," the scene is set for centralization. But if they reply first and foremost "I am a Virginian" or "I am a Buckeye," then it is difficult to imagine much centralization occurring.

We have very few systematic surveys of the objects of patriotic feeling in the United States and so we are forced to make impressionistic judgments of the kind of patriotism in existence at various points in history. We do know that in the early 1760's some people in North America began to think of themselves as Americans rather than British colonials, which process of identification was undoubtedly accelerated by the Revolutionary War. But what came out of the war is not quite clear: In the immediate postwar period did citizens think of themselves as citizens of the United States or citizens of Massachusetts, New York, Virginia, etc? Probably most of those who opposed the Constitution identified with the states rather than the nation. But the converse cannot be true for certainly many of the ardent federalists were also and consciously identified as state patriots in the next decade. Probably some sense of American nationality was created by and during the Revolution but also state nationality was created — and the latter was probably stronger than the former for some generations in at least some places in the country. Certainly in the South, where one condition of Civil War was a strong sense of state patriotism that could be manipulated by the small group of radicals who brought on the Montgomery Convention, state nationality was stronger than American nationality until long after the Civil War. On the other hand, for the winners, who had no reason to sentimentalize about a wound, the Civil War probably reduced identification with states and increased identification with the Union, in whose name the war was won.

Today there seems to be very little state nationalism left, outside of the South. Perhaps the two new states have more of it than any other non-Southern ones, owing doubtless to their long fight for statehood. Even some of the Southern patriotism seems weakened today, especially as black men, who have none, take a larger part in Southern affairs. This decline in identification with states seems to have accelerated in this century. Recently in a television interview H. V. Kaltenborn, whose career as a journalist reaches back to the 1890's, was asked the rather routine question: What is the main change you have seen in this country in your years of reporting? Kaltenborn unhesitatingly responded, "unification." He went on to elaborate that when he was young he thought of the United States as just that, a set of states united; but now he thought of it as a nation. Whether or not Kaltenborn is exactly correct about the timing of the new nationalism — the process is, of course, older than he and he saw only the latter part of it — there is no question that something of what Kaltenborn reported did in fact occur.

What influences, we may now ask, have brought about this gradual transfer of patriotism from state to nation? This is, of course, the grand question of nationalism; *i.e.*, what are its necessary and sufficient conditions? And what so many others have failed to answer, I cannot answer either, but I can suggest some of the conditions that seem to have been especially important:

1. *A high degree of mobility of labor.* A basic theme in American history is the long-continued existence of a frontier that drew heavily on already settled parts for its supply of labor. At least during the 19th century, the main pattern of migration was something like this: native free labor moved westward or, in the case of Southerners, westward and northwestward. Their place was taken, in the North, by immigrants from Europe and, in the South, by Negro slaves, whose breeding was a profitable business in the Southeast. Except in the South, this pattern of migration systematically weakened state patriotism. In the areas where European immigrants settled, state patriotism was weakened because the newcomers came to the new world to be Americans, not New Yorkers or Hoosiers. On the several frontiers state patriotism was weakened because the newcomers had old loyalties as well as new ones. Given pairs of state loyalties, it was easy to merge them into a national loyalty. The one place where this weakening process did not occur was the Southeast, always a relatively low-wage area and thus always an exporter, never an importer, of labor. But even there Southern regional patriotism at least came to equal state patriotism.

In this century the pattern of migration has been one of movement to metropolitan places. Interregional migration has been even greater than it was in the 19th century. But in one respect the pattern has continued, for the South has continued to be a net exporter of labor. Early in the century it contributed to the growth of the great cities of the Middle West; recently it has contributed to Texas and California. Thereby the state patriotism of those areas has been diluted and only the patriotism of the South is left unchanged.

2. *A high degree of mobility of leaders.* Although political leaders are typically home-town boys, leaders in nearly every other sphere of life are highly mobile and hence are without local territorial loyalties. As the control of American big business

has devolved from owners to managers a special managerial class has developed on a national basis. Its members trade in a national market, they are recruited on a national basis, and they transfer themselves frequently about the country as they rise in the corporate hierarchy. Even banking, once the most local of businesses, has spread into a national market in both transactions and personnel. In the learned professions, the educational system is such that mobility is encouraged. Schools of law and medicine, at least the ones with the best reputations, recruit and place their students on a national basis. Once well established, lawyers and physicians may not change residence; but, for the more successful figures in each profession, the probability is high that they have made a major change of residence at least once. The same kind of mobility is built into the educational system for engineers and research scientists, and this mobility is increased if they join the bureaucracies of either business or government. Even more marked is the mobility of college and university professors, for the structure of the profession is such that promotion is often dependent on mobility. The same dependence is characteristic in even greater degree of the clergy, and in hierarchical churches as well as congregational ones. And, whether exactly true or not, the popular stereotype of the journalist is that of a highly peripatetic man. Thus, both business leadership and intellectual leadership are now highly mobile in this country, rendering them highly impervious to the claims of state patriotism.

Only political leaders must stay in one place to rise in the world, and no longer is this true of all of them. Members of the federal bureaucracy both civil and military are of course moved about the country in the development of their careers. But increasingly the same is true of state and local bureaucrats. As functions such as social work, economic planning, and administrative management become professionalized, there turns out to be a national market for wardens, city managers, school officials, purchasing agents, etc. In short, states no longer expect state-oriented patriotism from some of their highest-paid officers. Against all this mobility among leaders generally and against the nationally oriented patriotism it permits, the happenstance of local orientation among elected officials cannot be expected to have much influence on the political culture generally. Hence follows a general indifference to the claims of state patriotism and a concentration on national loyalty.

3. *Military and quasi-military inculcation of patriotism.* A major requisite of military success is the inculcation throughout the military organization of loyalty to the unit of government it serves. The same function is also served by organizations of veterans, especially mass organizations. Given this function, then, it is quite important for the development of a national patriotism (1) that state military organizations mostly disappeared, indeed, were laughed out of existence in the 1830's and 1840's, (2) that a national mass army, followed by a national mass veterans' society developed during and after the Civil War, (3) that the Civil War also developed a mass regional army and veterans' organization, and (4) that the Spanish War and the two World Wars and the Korean War, all well within three generations, developed mass national armies and mass veterans' organizations, without any concomitant regionalism. The patriotism inculcated by both military and quasi-military organizations may be rather superficial and may be gauged to the lowest common denominator of understanding, but in this century, at least, it has been wholly national in focus.

4. *The existence of a common culture.* A common set of values in social life, morality, religion, ontology, etc. is not a necessary condition of federalism or even of centralization, but it is probably necessary to voluntary centralization wherein national loyalty gradually replaces loyalty to the constituent units.

The United States does not yet have a common culture, but it approaches closer to it each year. Furthermore, the main divisive elements in the culture are losing their geographic base in regionalism, so that the culture will in time homogenize itself.

If one is to believe the writers of belles-lettres, especially the humorists, there once existed several distinct types of American character: the Yankee, Southern aristocracy and Southern cracker, the Hoosier (who is something of a blend of the Yankee and the cracker), the plainsman, etc. Added to these during the latter part of the 19th century were special categories of immigrant types: the Irish laborer, the East-Side Jew, etc.

The striking thing about these regional and ethnic character types is that, assuming that they once existed, they are now disappearing.

In most of New England the Yankee has been swamped by Irish, Italian, and French-Canadian culture and out of the combination of these has come something that closely resembles the national culture. Only in the extreme back woods of western Massachusetts, coastal Maine, and rural Vermont and New Hampshire can one find remnants of the Yankee culture, and it is now so low-class socially that it has very little chance of surviving. Again the Hoosier type (not just in Indiana, but in the whole eastern part of the Middle West) is lost in a general American culture to which it contributed so heavily. (The general American dialect, the one used on national television in serious programs, is that spoken by educated people in Chicago, Indianapolis, Cleveland, etc.) The immigrant types may still exist in folk tales and humorous television programs, but each passing year makes it harder to find genuine representatives of the class. The grandchildren of the Irish laborer have merged into the general American middle class. Something of the same thing is happening to all other immigrant groups, although the Irish, who have been here longest, have assimilated furthest, except for the Germans, who were forced during two wars against Germany to shed any overt association with their ancestral culture.

My point is that the so-called American melting pot does indeed work as a melting pot, though not so swiftly as those who invented the simile perhaps supposed. Let me offer an analogy: Until recently many American cities had a distinctive type of architecture for middle-income housing. This type was usually entirely independent of national movements in architectural taste and was perpetuated chiefly because local builders could repeat it *ad nauseam* without going to the expense of having an architect create new floor plans and new utilization of materials. Thus, New York had its brownstones, Boston had its three-story tenements, Philadelphia–Baltimore–Washington had their row houses, Detroit its two-story, two-flat "upper incomes," Nashville its front-pillared Southern colonials, Chicago its three-story flats with rough-brick front facings and smooth-brick sides and rears, Denver its brick bungalows, San Francisco its pastel-colored, two-story houses with the garage on the first floor, etc., etc. Although in each city the middle-income housing was highly repetitious and hence tasteless in the minds of those who could afford to approximate a national taste in Italian villas or Dutch colonials or Tudor stuccos, still for those who could appreciate the wide regional variations there was a certain local charm in even so crude a design as the Detroit "upper income." Since at least World War II, however, local variations in middle-income housing have almost entirely disappeared, to be replaced by a national taste for Levittown-style bungalows, ranch houses, split levels, etc. If one examines the architectural styles of the recent suburbs of the cities I have mentioned, one finds no local variations but simply repetitions of the national styles.

As it is with so minor a matter as architectural taste, so I believe it is with much more important matters of character. The chance of local variation has declined. This may be a function of the mobility I have already discussed, but more likely it is a function of a general national effort to approximate a national middle-class culture, as set forth by movies, magazines, news agencies, television, etc. These media of public information and character-formation operate in a national market and must therefore conform to some sort of common denominator, which they have found in the middle-class culture and which they have had much to do with creating. Americans are said to strive for a middle-class position and public-opinion polls reveal that most do in fact believe they are nationally "middle class." Of course, all those who so believe model their behavior on what the culture suggests is the appropriate middle-class behavior so that local variations are wiped out.

There are doubtless many other influences that tend to transfer citizens' identification from state to nation. The ones I have listed and described are, however, of obvious importance and all are influential in the same direction, *viz.*, toward centralization. Thus it may be said that federalism in the United States is likely to be centralized further as time goes on.

5

Federalism outside the United States

THE FOREGOING survey of federalism in the United States has shown

(1) that administrative centralization and sharing have little to do with keeping the bargain;
(2) that the operation of political institutions, both those in the formal Constitution and those which have grown up outside of it, is what immediately maintains the bargain; and
(3) that standing behind these institutions is the popular sentiment of loyalty to (different levels of) government, which sentiment serves as a channel for development for centralizing or peripheralizing institutions.

In short, the fundamental feature of the maintenance of the bargain appears to be the third, next in importance comes the second, and finally comes the first, which, though often said to be most important, appears to be of only superficial significance for perpetuating federalism. To examine other instances of lasting federal bargains, let us, therefore, reverse the process and look first at the kinds of loyalties, then at the institutions, and finally at the administration of government in several of these systems.

I LOYALTIES IN SEVEN FEDERALISMS

Canada. Canadian federalism in considerably less centralized in tone than is federalism in the United States and the basic reason for this difference is doubtless the existence of a variety of non-federal loyalties, one of which is both intense and persistent. The great non-federal patriotism is the French Canadian identification with French Canadian culture. Though French Canadians have migrated all over eastern Canada and northeastern United States, still French Canada remains geographically identified with the province of Québec. From cursory examination this regional loyalty seems deeper than any such encountered in the United States. Like the present Southern regionalism in the United States, French-Canadian regionalism is based in great part on a resentment of past conquest and on a belief that the conquerers have continued to profit from the ancient conquest by contemporary economic exploitation. But unlike Southern regionalism, shame for the past and resentment for the present is reinforced daily by a consciously maintained difference in language and religion, as well as in social mores. Considering the active French Canadian resistance to drafts during World Wars I and II, it seems that this regionalism could still erupt into organized military resistance to encroachments from the central government. Southern regionalism in the United States no longer seems to have this potential strength.

In addition to French Canadian identification with Québec instead of Canada, Newfoundlanders also have a strong sense of local identification that weakens their attachment to Ottawa. Theirs was an independent dominion until the depression of the 1930's forced it to enter the Canadian federation. The sense of its separate history, reinforced by geographic isolation and its astute localistic politicians, creates a special local patriotism, which, however, time in the dominion will probably destroy. Again in western Canada there is a strong sense of geographic separation from Ottawa, which isolation encourages a series of provincial loyalties. These are probably weaker than the Newfoundland loyalty, but they are as numerous as the western provinces.

The effect of the existence of these several regional and provincial loyalties is that Canadian nationalism is a rather tenuous thing, composed chiefly of resentment and fear of Yankees and Yankee domination and without much enthusiasm for what the notion of Canada could itself mean in a positive sense.

Australia. In contrast to Canada — even in contrast to the United States — there is no intense regional identification in Australia. It is true that as recently as the mid-1930's western Australia proposed to separate from the Commonwealth and resume its former status as a crown colony; but this was more a maneuver in the perpetual haggling (over money) between the central and constituent governments than it was a genuine expression of regional separatism. It is true also that Australians have seldom voted, except under dire administrative necessity, for the frequently proposed (from the center) constitutional amendments to increase federal functions at the expense of the states; but this seems to express more a preference for local self-government than a provincial patriotism.

The divisions in Australian culture seem to be economic and religious with hardly any geographic base. Hence there also seems to be an Australian patriotism unobstructed by loyalties to states. Indeed, of all the federalisms now in existence, Australia seems less in need of appeasing subordinate patriotisms than any other government. One wonders, indeed, why they bother with federalism in Australia.

India. Many commentators on the new India observe that its most distinctive feature is the pervasiveness of conflict. Every village is split by factions; at every political level caste lines are lines of conflict; divisions of language, religion, color, and culture are all excuses for disagreement, bickering, rioting, and sedition. The broadest and most inclusive of these channels for conflict is the racial–linguistic–cultural division between the north and the south. The northerners speak Indo-European languages and are relatively light-skinned; the southerners speak Dravidian languages and are relatively darker. Since, especially in the south (where politicians and people are likely to feel abused by and inferior to the numerically superior north), the state boundaries largely coincide with linguistic boundaries, it follows that state patriotism means identification with the traditional culture of the region. It might have been (but was not, however) anticipated that independence would occasion a surge of regionalism and state-oriented nationalism. Very little of this existed in the era of British rule, probably because most politically conscious Hindus, at least, were united in their opposition to the British. Once their sole basis for agreement was removed, however, they promptly discovered intense regional loyalties. The central government (probably out of weakness) has pandered to these local identifications by creating state governments along linguistic boundaries, *e.g.*, Bombay, Madras, and Andhra, which were once based on British administrative boundaries but are now based on the limits of Maharastra-, Tamil-, and Telegu-speaking districts. Except for the Hindi-speaking area, which is divided among several states in the northwest, the Ganges valley, and the northern part of the central plateau, all the Indian states are also linguistic groupings. Naturally state patriotism flourishes in such an atmosphere and one can expect these local nationalisms to develop at a far faster rate than an All-Indian nationalism. In the Indian society there seems to be a reciprocal influence between the institutions of federalism and the underlying sentiment. The underlying sentiment has forced linguistic factions that find expression in the creation of subordinate governments to be loyal to, and this very loyalty in turn emphasizes the particularistic nature of the underlying sentiment.

Argentina. The early history of Argentina is characterized chiefly by disputes between Buenos Aires and the rest of the country. In general the opponents of the capital city were dominant in the 19th century, but in this century the governments seem to have relied mostly on the support of the urban and rural rich or the urban and rural poor. Hence, political controversies do not seem to have a geographic base and there is therefore little chance for local patriotism to develop. To an outsider it appears that local patriotisms, once strong, have declined in significance so that there is now no more reason for federalism in Argentina than there is in Australia.

Brazil. It is quite otherwise in Brazil. Unlike Argentina, where there is only one great city and where provincial loyalties must look backward to an earlier culture and an earlier economy, in Brazil there are several great cities and a number of centers of regional culture. Unlike Argentina, which has a relatively homogeneous economy based on cattle, wheat, and industrialization of the La Plata basin, Brazil has a highly diversified economy (even though coffee is popularly supposed to dominate). Brazil has always been organized into a series of seaports with hinterlands, each of which forms an obvious economic and cultural region around which loyalties can be created. These loyalties have existed from colonial days and not until the last generation (during the dictatorship of Vargas) did any national leader attempt to submerge them into a national patriotism. Vargas succeeded only in small part and subsequent leaders have not outshone him.

Germany. German nationalism, a product of both 19th-century romanticism and 19th-century *real-politik*, was resented throughout the period of the empire by, especially, South Germans as a device of Prussia to dominate all German-speaking populations. But the largely unobstructed inculcation of a German-centered patriotism during the last hundred years has so dulled the edge of this resentment that today there seems to be as small a number of local patriotisms in Germany as in Australia. One doubts if the imperial federalism would have been revived for the Bonn government if it had not been greatly desired by the chief occupying power and if it had not seemed expedient as a way of ultimately reattracting East Germany.

Soviet Union. Although the majority of people in the Soviet Union speak Russian and the majority of these identify themselves as Russian, there are many lesser language–culture groups that together make up a significant non-Russian minority. The imperial method for dealing with this minority was to attempt to Russianize it. Naturally, this policy occasioned deep resentment among all those groups who were at all conscious of what was being done to them. Indeed, it was a self-defeating policy, for it increased the intensity of just those emotions it was supposed to eliminate. Under Soviet federalism the policy has been to some degree reversed. With some hesitations, minority nationalities have been encouraged to develop their language, literature, and local patriotism so long as none of these have run counter to the concerns of the Communist party. The theory behind this policy was that, in the absence of repression, local patriotism could and would, if guided by the party, turn gradually into a Soviet patriotism. In some instances it actually seems to have worked out this way, especially when, as in the instance of Armenia, the local patriotism had been persistently repressed and persecuted by all governments but the Soviet. In other instances, *e.g.*, the Volga Germans, the policy seems to have intensified an anti-Soviet nationalism. Hence it is difficult to assess the state of local patriotisms in the Soviet Union today. Whether they have on the whole diminished or intensified we cannot say, but we do know that they continue to exist.

II INSTITUTIONS OF SEVEN FEDERALISMS

Canada. On the paper of the British North America Act, Canada appears to be a highly centralized federalism; in fact it is not, which is a paradox to be explained. The framers of this Act, writing at the end of the Civil War in the United States, attempted to avoid the defects that the war had revealed in the older federalism. So they tried to revise some of the most peripheralizing features, especially in the allocation of functions among the governments and in the structure of the Senate. In the federalism of the United States the constitutional assumption is that authority not granted to the central government remains in the constituent governments. (This is the reason why each addition to the functions of the central government in this country has occasioned so much legalistic debate.) In the Canadian version, however, the authority not granted to the constituent units remains in the center, an allocation that presumably makes the central government stronger in relation to the provinces than the federal government in the United States is in relation to the states. Again, in our federalism, the Senate was selected by state governments and senators were presumably responsible to them, although, as we have already seen, this presumption was half gone by the time of the Civil War. In Canada, on the other hand, though seats in the Senate were allocated to provinces, the appointment of Senators was assigned to the Governor-General, which meant of course the Prime Minister. Hence, the Senators never have had a sense of representing provinces and the Canadian Senate has never been regarded as a bulwark of states' rights. (Indeed, since it has generally been used to give pensions to elderly politicians, the Canadian Senate has never counted for much of anything.)

Superficially, therefore, the Canadian system is highly centralized. But, looking beyond the formal prescriptions of the Constitution, there are some highly peripheralizing extra-constitutional institutions. One of these, the use of the judicial committee of the Privy Council in Great Britain to serve as a final court of appeal in matters of constitutional interpretation, was abandoned in 1949. But for the preceding seventy-five years the judicial committee served as a peripheralizing device. Not only did its personnel generally adhere to the kind of social philosophy that in the United States produced the doctrine of dual federalism but also the judges in London tended to have a highly unrealistic view of federalism in general and of Canadian federalism in particular. Hence, they systematically curtailed the authority of the central government, modeling the Canadian federation after the United States rather than after the indigenous plans as expressed in the British North America Act. Although the right of appeal to the judicial committee has now been abolished in favor of a national Supreme Court that can be expected to be more responsive to Canadian needs and the pull of centralization, the effect of the long dominance by the judicial committee is that many functions ordinarily performed in the United States by the central government are performed in Canada by the provinces.

More important for peripheralization is the structure of the political party system. As Steven Muller puts it,[1] there are two

[1] *Federalism and the Party System in Canada* (mimeographed, paper presented at American Political Science Association meeting, St. Louis, Mo., 1961).

layers of political parties in Canada, one at the dominion level and the other at the provincial level. In the dominion system, there are two national parties (Liberals and Conservatives) and several splinter parties. Most voters in most provinces vote for candidates of one of the two dominion-wide parties in dominion elections and the control of the central government has always been in the hands of one of these two national parties. But at the provincial level the party system is very different. Typically, in the provinces one of the national parties faces not the other national party, but a strong local party that appears to be a splinter party on the national scene. Only in Ontario and the Maritimes is the national party system reproduced on the provincial level. Elsewhere, the dominant provincial parties are the Social Credit party and the New Democratic party (Socialist) in the west generally, and various French parties in Québec. Furthermore, the Liberal party in Newfoundland has almost no relationship with the national Liberal party and is simply a vehicle for Newfoundland nationalism. The effect of this double system is that the national party in control of the national government cannot rely on the majority of provincial governments under the control of provincial parties to follow the lead of the national government. Even within the Liberal party, provincial prime ministers look to Liberal leaders in Ottawa, not for leadership, but for bargaining concessions of exactly the same sort that might be gained by Social Credit or Union Nationale provincial ministries. And there is something to bargain about. The financial system as it has worked out over the past century consists of agreements by the provinces to give up their taxing power to the center in return for subsidies. Since the tradition supposes that the amount of subsidy is variable, the government in Ottawa is constantly negotiating with provincial governments about the amount. Naturally the intensity of negotiation is greatest just prior to dominion elections. Pragmatic politicians in provincial Canada seem to have realized that the governments of the so-called splinter parties (really the governing parties in the provinces) are better in this negotiation than are governments of the same party as the one that governs in Ottawa. Hence they have maintained the system of national and local parties to facilitate local bargaining for national money. This is what chiefly peripheralizes the Canadian system.

Australia. The Australian system is, like the Canadian, much less centralized than the system of the United States, but for somewhat different reasons. To begin with, the Australian system was intended as an almost peripheralized federalism. Its framers' image of the United States came from an era in which the Supreme Court was systematically endeavoring to undo the centralization occasioned by the Civil War. Whereas the Canadian framers looked at the horror of the Civil War and sought to minimize the danger of its replication by centralizing their system more than that of the United States, the Australian framers interpreted the degree of centralization in the United States as just about right and so copied our system as it was in 1900. They avoided the most peripheralizing feature of the earlier system in the United States; *i.e.*, a Senate responsible to state governments, largely because that institution had largely disappeared by 1900. The Australian Senate was to be popularly elected in states in about the same way as the United States Senate is. On the other hand, they copied the notion of a Supreme Court to adjudicate controversies over the division of functions and they assigned residual (*i.e.*, unlisted) functions to the states, just as in the United States system. As a consequence the Australian system, on paper and in fact, has been less centralized than ours throughout its history.

But this decentralization is not based on formal constitutional provisions alone. As in Canada, it is also based on local peculiarities in the systems of political parties and finance. The Australian party system consists of three national parties, Liberal, Country, and Labour, which are also the parties of the states. On the national level, Liberal and Country usually align against Labour, so that something of a two-party system exists. But on the state level, though two-party systems usually exist, they are not the same systems as those found on the national level. Thus in New South Wales the Labour party that usually dominates the state government is not the same ideologically as the federal Labour party. Indeed, twice in a generation the NSW Labour party has been split when the federal Labour party has sought to bring it to heel. Both times the federal party has eventually won, but only at the cost of alienating the largest state Labour party for a considerable length of time. Quite clearly NSW Labour has opposed the federal Labour party more often than it has obeyed it in the last thirty-five years. On the other hand, the Tasmanian Labour party, which has governed the smallest state for most of the last generation, has been ideologically and personally cooperative with the federal Labour party. Other state–federal relationships within the Labour party vary between these extremes. In the Liberal and Country parties, dramatic fights as in the Labour party between federal and state parties have not occurred; but both parties, especially the Country party, are devoted to an ideal of decentralization, so that the federal party has usually preferred to accommodate itself to the state leadership. Hence, there has been little reason for such fights to occur. In sum, where the Labour party has aspired to centralization and failed, the Liberal and Country parties have accepted the fact of decentralization. As a result of both cases, the party system has been quite decentralized.

And this is quite as it should be, given the financial relationships between the state and federal governments. As in Canada, the state governments are the main spenders (for purposes other than defense) of money raised by the central government. As in Canada also, the negotiations between the states and the center on financial questions are fairly constant and quite reasonably the voters in states are happy to pit their state governments against the federal government in arm's-length bargaining. They appear to realize that really disciplined national parties would destroy state advantages in bargaining.

India. Throughout its brief history India has appeared to have a highly centralized federalism. For one thing its constitution, written in an era of economic planning and welfare statism, gives rather greater administrative duties to the central government than do the older federal constitutions in the American-Commonwealth tradition. For another thing, its constitution incorporates the device, adopted from similar devices in Argentina and Brazil, of federal intervention to govern states that fail to perform satisfactorily (when, of course, the federal government is judge of what is satisfactory performance). Third, it has been governed since independence, both at the center and in most states, by a quite centralized party. Beyond these constitutional facts are the administrative details, which seem to support the interpretation of a high degree of centralization: the central government controls most of the economy by means of central economic planning; the central government has twice taken over the government of states it believed to be mismanaged; and the national leadership of the Congress party has succeeded both in forcing local nominating committees to nominate candidates who are locally disliked and in persuading the voters to elect these candidates simply because of the party label. By reason of all these details, therefore, one would today be justified in describing Indian federalism as highly centralized.

But beneath this simple façade of centralization lies a somewhat more complex reality. Ever since independence, India has been governed by a revolutionary party still structured by the pre-independence agreement on the urgency of unity. Through the entire period of independence this revolutionary party has been led by a great revolutionary leader, who has outlived all his rivals of pre-independence days. Under Nehru, the Congress party has so far been able to impose national discipline on local units and thereby India has achieved governmental centralization. But, as all observers of the Indian political scene continually inquire, "After Nehru, what?" Surely the particular brand of centralization he has brought to the system can no longer continue to exist. Lesser leaders will probably not be able to maintain discipline in the Congress — indeed recently even Nehru appears to be losing his ability to do so. And if Congress should be superseded by another party or coalition, national control of state politics will surely disappear, for all the rest of the parties — even the Communist — are decentralized in character.

We must, I believe, reserve judgment on the nature of the Indian system. With a non-Congress, or at least a non-Nehru, government, India might turn out to be quite decentralized. On the other hand, the dangers of decentralization are so great (from the point of view of maintaining a viable nation) that it seems equally possible that a non-Congress government might be a military dictatorship of the sort to be found in Pakistan.

Argentina. Despite social and economic conditions encouraging peripheralization and the domination of political life by local caudillos and landlords, Argentina has a long tradition of highly centralized institutions based both on provisions of the Constitution and on the structure of political parties. The crucial constitutional provision is that which permits national intervention in the government of provinces. It is copied from the guarantee in the Constitution of the United States of republican government to the states. Though this provision has not been used here (although it might have been used to justify reconstruction after the Civil War), it has been used frequently in Argentina, averaging nearly twice a year over the last century. When the federal government intervenes, its agent removes the elected officials (governor, provincial legislators, and federal deputies) and judges, calls a special election, and then turns the government of the province over to the products of this election. Since the elections are invariably policed by the national army, the candidates sponsored by the federal president invariably win. This system of course provides that the national government can, if it chooses, control the governments of the provinces.

In addition to this legal method, the structure of the party system has provided — at least in recent years — for easy central coercion of provincial governments. In the 19th and early 20th centuries, the parties were essentially coalitions of local caudillos, which made it difficult for one to dominate the others. But in more recent times, with the rise of mass parties, it has been possible for the caudillo also to be a charismatic dictator such as Perón.

These avenues for central coercion of the provinces complement each other: the legal technique has worked to induce national control of the provinces when the governing officials at the center have lacked effective partisan control, whereas effective partisan control obviates the need for intervention. Hence it follows that Argentina has, despite its size and passionate federalist tradition, appeared (especially in the last generation) to be a quite centralized federalism.

Brazil. Brazil's constitutional provisions on intervention are closely similar to Argentina's and the United States', but they were seldom used prior to the Vargas regime, at which time the dictator's attempt to unify the government took the form of both a national party and intervention in states. Usually, however, Brazil could be said to have been less centralized than Argentina, largely because, prior to Vargas, national leadership seldom felt strong enough to restrain the peripheralism of the Brazilian tradition.

Germany. In part of its constitutional structure the German system appears decentralized since the Länder cabinets directly select the members of the national upper house, which has some legislative power, although the chancellor is not responsible to it, On the other hand, the national legislature has constitutional authority to legislate in a far wider variety of substantive areas than do most other national legislatures of federalisms. In this way, the constitution appears to be centralized. Still the federal government does not directly administer programs in many of the areas of action about which it legislates, so that again the constitution appears decentralized. As a consequence of this mixture of features most writers have been confused about how to classify the Bonn federalism. Given the fact that German federalism is the only one in the world that does not derive its structure from the tradition of the United States, it is not surprising that this confusion exists in the minds of scholars accustomed to using American legal categories. Fortunately for this discussion, however, the significant centralizing feature for German federalism is, as in the other instances so far examined, the structure of the party system. Under the Bonn government's first chancellor, the Christian Democratic Union, which has always been the governing party at the center, was rigidly centralized. Nominations, even for Länder offices, have apparently been rigidly controlled by the party leadership; and, since organizational control leads to policy control, the German federalism has clearly been quite centralized.

The reasons for this seem, however, to be more personal than constitutional: Adenauer's leadership depended on his personal position in his party and in his relationship with the occupying powers. Whether the partisan centralization he imposed can survive his disappearance from the political scene is, it seems to me, entirely unpredictable. If the central leadership of the CDU can retain its hold on the party — and the electoral system is such as to encourage such a hold — and if the CDU can maintain itself in office long enough to make partisan centralization an accepted pattern, then it is probable that the present centralization will survive. But if either of these conditions does not exist, then the decentralizing features of the constitution (*e.g.*, the structure of the Bundesrat, the assignment of the administration of federal statutes to the Länder, etc.) are likely to decentralize the whole system.

Soviet Union. In the Soviet constitution, the method of selecting officials of the constituent units is at least as decentralized as in the United States, the distribution of governmental functions between the All-Union governments and the governments of the Soviet republics is at least as decentralized as in India, and the formal guarantees of the independence of the two levels of government are at least as viable on paper as they are in Canada. Yet no one, not even Soviet scholars, would for a moment suggest that the Soviet federalism is decentralized. Indeed, throughout its history, except for a brief few months immediately after its inception, the Soviet system has been as fully centralized as dictatorships in unitary governments. The explanation of this paradox is simple: under the Soviet constitution and in political practice the only legal party in the Soviet Union is the Communist party, which is itself organized on a strictly hierarchical basis. The possible effect of the formal guarantees of republic integrity is thus completely submerged by the effect of extreme centralization in the structure of the single political party.

III ADMINISTRATIVE CENTRALIZATION

A thorough examination of the kind and degree of administrative centralization in seven federalisms would require far more space than is available in this brief survey. But the relevance of administrative centralization to the maintenance of the bargain may be grasped from the table of relative expenditures by the several levels of government in selected recent years (Table 5.1).

In this table, part I is a comparison for the United States and Canada of expenditures at three levels of government (national, state or provincial, and local). Part II is a comparison for the United States, Canada, and India of expenditures at the national and state or provincial levels. Part III is a comparison for the United States, Australia, Germany, and the Soviet Union of expenditures at the national level with expenditures at the state (or Länder or Republic) and local levels combined.

Nothing particularly definitive appears from Table 5.1. Nearly all observers, including Communists, would agree that the Soviet Union is far more centralized than the United States and indeed that the original guarantees to the constituent republics have not been kept by the Soviet government. Yet administratively it is somewhat less centralized than the United States. Similarly, most observers would agree that Canada is a more peripheralized federalism than the United States, that Québec and French Canada are allowed greater leeway than any dissident region in the United States, and that the guarantees to the provinces have been much more faithfully respected in Canada than in the United States. Yet administratively it is almost as centralized as the United States. Again, Germany is, so most observers insist, a more centralized federalism than the United States; but administratively it appears to be peripheralized. This appearance is, of course, a function of Germany's peculiar federalism in which most administration is delegated to the Länder. Still the very fact of the appearance suggests that administrative centralization or decentralization has very little to do with whether or not a federal government is centralized or peripheralized.

IV THE MEASUREMENT OF FEDERALISM

The foregoing survey of the kinds of forces that maintain the federal bargain suggests that many influences commonly thought to be significant either for centralization or

Table 5.1 ANNUAL EXPENDITURES IN SIX FEDERALISMS BY LEVELS OF GOVERNMENT FOR SELECTED RECENT YEARS

<table>
<tr><th rowspan="2">Country, year, and monetary unit</th><th colspan="4">Expenditures</th><th rowspan="2">Percentage of total expenditures made by central government</th></tr>
<tr><th>Central government</th><th>Constituent governments (e.g., states)</th><th>Local governments (e.g., towns)</th><th>Total for all levels</th></tr>
<tr><td>I</td><td></td><td></td><td></td><td></td><td></td></tr>
<tr><td>United States, 1960, billions of dollars</td><td>76.5</td><td>17.9</td><td>33.9</td><td>128.3</td><td>60%</td></tr>
<tr><td>Canada, 1959, billions of dollars</td><td>5.6</td><td>2.5</td><td>1.9</td><td>10.0</td><td>57%</td></tr>
<tr><td>II</td><td></td><td></td><td></td><td></td><td></td></tr>
<tr><td>United States, 1960</td><td>76.5</td><td>17.9</td><td></td><td>94.4</td><td>81%</td></tr>
<tr><td>Canada, 1960</td><td>5.6</td><td>2.5</td><td></td><td>8.1</td><td>70%</td></tr>
<tr><td>India, 1960 millions of rupees</td><td>17.1</td><td>10.7</td><td></td><td>27.8</td><td>61%</td></tr>
<tr><td>III</td><td></td><td></td><td></td><td></td><td></td></tr>
<tr><td>United States, 1960</td><td>76.5</td><td colspan="2">51.8</td><td>128.3</td><td>60%</td></tr>
<tr><td>Australia, 1960, millions of pounds</td><td>1.1</td><td colspan="2">0.9</td><td>2.0</td><td>55%</td></tr>
<tr><td>Germany, 1959, millions of marks</td><td>30.7</td><td colspan="2">47.5</td><td>78.2</td><td>38%</td></tr>
<tr><td>Soviet Union, 1960, billions of new roubles</td><td>17.1</td><td colspan="2">18.2</td><td>35.5</td><td>49%</td></tr>
</table>

peripheralization are relatively insignificant. Our problem now is to assess relative degrees of significance and this is, of course, a problem of measurement. Thus, a discussion of the measurement of federalism is really a summary of this chapter and the two preceding ones.

Let us start with this question: Suppose one wishes to assert that federalism A is more or less centralized (or peripheralized) than federalism B. Or suppose one wishes to assert that federalism A at time t_0 is more or less centralized (or peripheralized) than at time t_1. What considerations would necessarily enter into such assertions?

The preliminary question is, of course, what are the forces one ought to assess to determine the degree of centralization or peripheralization? Should one measure, for example, the degree of influence on national decisions by legislative houses elected from the constituent units? Or should one measure the range of areas of action assigned to the central and constituent governments respectively, etc.?

In Chapters 3, 4, and 5 the variables mentioned as influencing the degree of centralization include: (1) the kind of assignment of areas of policy formation to the two levels of government, (2) the existence or non-existence of some kind of formal control by constituent governments over the decisions of the central government (*e.g.*, election of some officers of the central government by constituent governments, as in the original United States Senate), (3) the kind of party organization in the two levels of government, (4) the degree of citizens' loyalty to each of the two levels of government, (5) the kind of assignment of administrative responsibility to the two levels of government. Let us consider each of these five variables to determine whether or not it should be taken into account in constructing a measure of federalism. Such a consideration amounts to asking about each one what, if anything, it contributes to the maintenance of the federal bargain.

It is easy, I believe, to show that most of these supposed variables are only indirectly relevant to variations in federalism. The detailed analysis in Chapter 3 of the assignment of areas of policy formation indicates that such variation as is possible in this assignment has little to do with variations in centralization and peripheralization. Thus in the period from 1790 to 1860 the assignment both centralized and peripheralized, whereas the decision-making process as a whole tended to become somewhat more centralized. It seems probable that variations in assignment are pragmatically determined by the technological needs of administration, that in any particular area policy is made by the lowest level at which reasonably effective action can be anticipated. Thus transfers of assignment, which appear to involve centralization, may reflect no more than a changing technology that has, *e.g.*, expanded markets to the point that local governments can no longer regulate them. Or again, transfers that appear to involve peripheralization may reflect no more than the correction of a misunderstood and undesired centralization in the original constitutional scheme (as in Canada from 1880-1940). Still other transfers may in fact reflect genuine changes in federalism; but it seems likely that when they do so reflect they are concomitant but not necessary variations. Thus, such transfers may be occasioned by the same fundamental forces that also occasion centralization and peripheralization, as when a decline in provincialism and a strengthening of the national parties lead to centralization. If the transfers of function always and only proceeded from forces that changed the federal relationship, then one might use a measure on the transfers as a measure of federalism. But since the transfers often appear to be unrelated to the structure of federalism, a measure on the transfers tells us nothing certain about federalism.

Similarly, the assignment of administrative responsibility seems to imply nothing about the basic structure of federalism. As the analysis earlier in this chapter indicated, the division of administrative duty may reflect no more than administrative convenience (as in the Soviet Union) or it may be a consequence of adventitious increases in the significance of particular functions. Thus the military function may at times become extraordinarily important, overshadowing all else; yet, in the experience of the United States at least, such predominance never seems to have permanently affected the federal relationship.

Likewise, the existence of formal controls by the constituent governments over decision-making bodies of the central government seems to imply very little about the structure of federalism. It is certainly true that basic changes in the formal controls are reflected in the process of decision making. But it is also true (as, for example, in Brazil, Argentina, and Mexico) that the degree of decentralization in decision making can vary, indeed even that the guarantees to constituent units can effectually disappear, without any change in the formal controls. Hence, one cannot say that institutional structure varies with the realities of federalism.

Turning to the influence of the degree of citizen loyalty to the two levels of government, it is apparent that one reason for maintaining a peripheralized federalism is to allow freedom of action to the constituent governments when the citizens have a deeper loyalty to them than to the center. Hence one indication of peripheralization is the existence of abiding local loyalties. But some peripheralized decision-making systems do not exhibit intense loyalties to constituent units, so the relationship between provincialism and peripheralized federalism is not isomorphic. In Australia there are no intense provincialisms, but the federalism is almost peripheralized, whereas in the Soviet Union there are numerous nationalisms (some of which may be intense) but the federalism is fully centralized.

At least four of the five forces presumably influencing the degree of centralization are, it appears, not closely enough related to constitutional reality to serve as measures of the federal relationship. But what about the fifth force; *i.e.*, the kind of party organization in the two levels of government? In this case it seems that a fairly consistent relationship exists, a relationship that can be summarized thus: The federal relationship is centralized according to the degree to which the parties organized to operate the central government control the parties organized to operate the constituent governments. This amounts to the assertion that the proximate cause of variations in the degree of centralization (or peripheralization) in the constitutional structure of a federalism is the variation in degree of party centralization.

There are strong *a priori* arguments for the validity of this assertion of a causal connection. Suppose the officials of the central government wish to centralize to a degree greater than the formal constitution of the federalism contemplates (*i.e.*, suppose these officials wish to break the federal bargain in their favor). Suppose further that these officials are the leaders of a party that also operates constituent governments through subordinate leaders. That is, suppose the parties are highly centralized. Then, it would seem that all the constitutional and institutional prohibitions guaranteeing constituent governments against revision of the federal bargain would be ineffectual. If, on the other hand, the officials of the central government do not have partisan supporters operating the constituent governments, they may expect some opposition to their breaking of the guarantees. Whether or not the opposition is strong enough to maintain the bargain depends of course on a variety of institutional circumstances. But whether or not the opposition occurs at all seems to depend initially on a partisan difference between the central and constituent leadership.

There is even some empirical evidence supporting the notion that the degree of partisan unity between the constituent and central governments is closely related to changes in the federal relationship. In another place,[2] Schaps and I devised a measure of the degree of partisan disharmony between the two levels of government and, when we correlated the index of disharmony by eight recent bienniums in the United States with the absolute amount of litigation between the two levels of governments in the Supreme Court, we obtained a coefficient of correlation of about +0.8, which is within the 2 per cent level of confidence. This finding suggests that to a very high degree variations in the federal relationship, especially variations in the ability of constituent governments to conflict with the central government, depend on variations in partisan relationships between the two levels.

What is suggested by this finding about a barely visible feature of federalism in the United States is also suggested by a much grosser observation of other systems. Thus, consider the federalisms in category A mentioned in the beginning of Chapter 4; that is, the federalisms in which the central government is invariably able to overawe the constituent governments, *viz.* Mexico, the Soviet Union, and Yugoslavia. One other characteristic these

[2] William H. Riker and Ronald Schaps, "Disharmony in Federal Government," *Behavioral Science*, Vol. 2 (1957) pp. 276-90.

three political systems share is the fact that one and only one political party rules all levels of government. If the theory just set forth is correct, it is the feature of one-partyism that causes the rupture of the federal bargain. At the other extreme, consider the federalisms in category C; that is, those in which constituent governments can overawe the center, whereas central officials cannot overawe them. There are relatively few governments in this category (since it verges on the complete collapse of the federal bargain), but Nigeria offers at least one contemporary example. If the theory here set forth is correct, there should be many parties in Nigeria and the national levels of these parties should have little or no influence over the constituent levels. Such in fact is the case, for the main party leaders prefer to hold office in the constituent governments rather than in the central government. Thus at both extremes of variation in the federal relationship, it appears that the variations in partisanship are causally related to variations in federalism. Since in the instance of the United States, which is clearly in category B, the same causal relationship appears, one easily infers that the same causal connection is valid for all systems in all categories.

The exact nature of this causal connection can best be examined by asking how to measure the federal relationship according to the partisan variation. Once one asks this question, it is immediately apparent that there are involved two kinds of relationships between parties at the two levels: (1) the degree to which one party controls both levels of government; and (2) the degree to which each potential governing party at the national level controls its partisan associates at the level of constituent governments. An exhaustive consideration of these possibilities may be obtained from Table 5.2, in which the rows concern the degree to which the governing party controls both levels and the columns concern the degree of party discipline at the central and constituent levels. (Note: no differentiation in discipline among parties is considered, since it is assumed that, if one party is disciplined, others gradually come to be.) The intersection of the rows and columns then states the category of centralization (or peripheralization) to which the particular federalism that satisfies these conditions belongs. The assignment of a particular federalism to either rows one and two or three and four can be estimated by such simple measures as the average frequency of turnover in partisan control, modified, of course, for statement as a probability measure. The assignment of a particular federalism to either rows one and three or rows two and four can be estimated by a measure of the previous experience of the federalism about the degree of similarity of party control at the two levels.[3] Finally, the assignment of a particular federalism to any one of the four columns can be estimated by a measure of some feature of party discipline, such as voting in the legislature. The Rice index of cohesion on roll calls, for example, can be averaged for parties over a series of roll calls in both national and constituent legislatures.

The entries in Table 5.2 represent my judgment of where each set of partisan circumstances leads to a location on the range between almost complete centralization (*i.e.*, A) and almost complete peripheralization (*i.e.*, D). The entries can be rationalized as follows:

(1,1) (read: "row 1, column 1") This is the intersection of complete discipline at both levels with low probability either that the party in control of the central government will change or that the party controlling central government will fail to control a majority of

[3] One measure of the degree of similarity is found in William H. Riker and Ronald Schaps, "Disharmony in Federal Government," *Behavioral Science*, Vol. 2 (1957) pp. 276-90. The index of disharmony is calculated thus: For any party (or governing coalition of parties) whose power index in the national government is greater than 0.5, one minus the power index of that party (or parties) in the sum of the constituent governments is the partisan disharmony in a federalism. This index in turn depends on the Shapley-Shubik power index (see L. S. Shapley and Martin Shubik, "A Method of Evaluating the Distribution of Power in a Committee System," *American Political Science Review*, Vol. 48 (1954) pp. 787-92) which is the chance that a particular member of a legislature has to be the last added member of a minimum winning coalition over the sum of such chances for all members. The power index for a party is, of course, the chance that its members in a legislature, which in the United States usually includes three houses (upper house, lower house, executive), have to be the last added member of a winning coalition over the sum of all such chances. The index of federal disharmony reveals the degree to which the central and constituent governments differ in partisan control.

Table 5.2 DEGREE OF CENTRALIZATION OF FEDERALISMS

				Degree of Party Regularity			
				National level *disciplined*		National level *not disciplined*	
				Constituent level		Constituent level	
				disciplined	*not disciplined*	*disciplined*	*not disciplined*
Chance that party in control of central government will be replaced by another party	$pr < 0.5$	Chance that more than half the control of constituent governments will be in the hands of parties other than the party in control of the national government	$pr < 0.5$	A –	A	C +	B –
	$pr < 0.5$		$pr \geqq 0.5$	B	B +	C	C
	$pr \geqq 0.5$		$pr < 0.5$	B	B +	C	C +
	$pr \geqq 0.5$		$pr \geqq 0.5$	B –	B –	D	D +

constituent governments. Except for the strength of parties at the constituent level to resist, this seems the ideal circumstance for the transfer of all decision making to the center.

(1,2) The modification of (1,1) involved in (1,2) is simply the weakening of partisan control of constituent governments. Presumably this would increase the likelihood of the transfer of decision making to the center, for party leadership at the constituent level would be too weak to resist it effectually.

(1,3) In this case the lack of discipline at the center presumably allows the disciplined constituent units of the centrally governing party to control decisions even though the same party has a good chance at permanent control of both central and constituent governments.

(1,4) Although neither level is disciplined in this case, still the continuity of control at both levels seems to direct me to place this intersection in the B category, at least marginally.

(2,1) Although parties are well disciplined at both levels, the chance that a majority of the constituent governments will be partisanly different from the likely controller of the central government admits also the chance of some independence of action by the constituent governments.

(2,2) This case differs from the previous one only in the fact that parties at the constituent level are less well disciplined than at the national level. This difference seems to permit less efficient utilization of the chance for independence.

(2,3)
(2,4) } The lack of discipline at the national level coupled with discipline at the constituent level and weakness in the national party's hold on office in constituent governments indicate category C for both cases.

(3,1) Even though the governing party's hold on national office is insecure, its discipline, coupled with the assurance of the similarity of partisan control at both levels, suggests the possibility of considerable centralization.

(3,2) The possibility of centralization is increased in comparison with (3,1) by the lack of discipline at the constituent level.

(3,3) The lack of discipline at the national level coupled with discipline at the constituent level effectually prevents centralization, even though the same party governs at both levels.

(3,4) The difference between this case and the previous one is the absence of discipline at the constituent level; and this absence permits the similarity of partisan control to work more effectively for centralization.

(4,1) The only difference between this and case (3,1) is in the likelihood of partisan similarity in control of the two levels.

(4,2) Given the weakness in control by the governing party at the national level, the lack of discipline at the constituent level does not seem to be enough to differentiate this case from (4,1).

(4,3) The insecurity of the national governing party coupled with discipline at the constituent level seems the ideal setting for peripheralization.

(4,4) This case differs from the preceding one only in reducing the discipline of parties at the constituent level, which presumably reduces the efficiency of constituent-level parties at inducing peripheralization.

V SUMMARY: WHAT MAINTAINS FEDERALISM?

Chapters 3, 4, and 5 have been devoted to a search for the circumstances that keep the federal bargain alive after the original military–diplomatic considerations that call it forth have ceased to be operative. The conclusions may be stated thus:

1. The division and sharing of administrative responsibilities, which is often said to be at the heart of federal arrangements, has little or nothing to do with maintaining the bargain. In the United States such centralization as has occurred seems to have been occasioned by technological considerations and to have had little effect, one way or another, on the bargain. Certainly in the period most crucial for its maintenance, some functions were centralized and others peripheralized, which suggests the genuine irrelevance of this consideration. In seven other federalisms there seems to be no rhyme or reason for the degree of administrative centralization except administrative traditions and convenience. Again there seems to be no connection between centralization or peripheralization in decision making and centralization or peripheralization of administrative functions. (This conclusion vitiates a vast amount of scholarly inquiry about, especially, American federalism, much of which inquiry has investigated the relationship be-

tween centralization of functions and the supposed demise of federalism.)

2. It is true that federalism is maintained by the existence of dual citizen loyalties to the two levels of government. But this assertion is almost a tautology. Federalism means the existence of two levels each to some degree able to decide questions independently. Without loyalty to each of the two levels, both could not continue to exist. Besides being tautological, this statement tells us little about the degree of centralization in a federalism.

Many writers wish to utter a much stronger companion statement: Federalism is maintained by the existence of dissident provincial patriotisms. Although this sentence appears to be true in many instances (*e.g.*, the United States, where a gradual decline in provincialism seems to accompany some centralization, Canada, Brazil, etc.), it does not appear to be true of Australia or Argentina, where provincial patriotisms seem to be relatively weak.

Hence, in a larger sense one can say the federal bargain is maintained by loyalties to both levels, but one cannot always say that it is maintained because of the need to satisfy a dissident provincialism such as that of the South in the United States or of French Canadians in Canada.

3. Whatever the general social conditions, if any, that sustain the federal bargain, there is one institutional condition that controls the nature of the bargain in all the instances here examined and in all others with which I am familiar. This is the structure of the party system, which may be regarded as the main variable intervening between the background social conditions and the specific nature of the federal bargain.

4. It is theoretically possible but practically difficult to measure the structure of the party system.

6

Is the federal bargain worth keeping?

UP TO THIS point this interpretation of federalism has been as simply descriptive as I have been able to keep it. The questions of whether or not federalism is superior to its contemporary alternative, unitary government, or its previous alternative, imperialism; of whether or not federalism makes for good government or the good life; of whether or not federalism is an effective instrument of political integration — all these I have tried to keep out of the discussion in order to concentrate on the descriptive questions: What occasions federalism and what maintains it?

But most of the interest in federalism, both academic and popular, is about the further question: Is federalism worth keeping? And so in this final chapter we shall consider this moral question, not attempting to answer it but rather attempting to indicate some of the considerations that may properly enter into the answer.

Please note that I put the question "Is federalism worth keeping?" not "Is federalism worth starting?" If the argument in

Chapters 1 and 2 has any validity at all, the latter question is trivial. In the drive for territorial expansion at the breakup of empire, one either needs to use the federal device to expand or one does not. Normative considerations presumably do not enter into calculation, once the decision to expand has been made. (Of course, that decision is itself normative; but, once it is made, the decision on the procedure of expansion is purely technical. Since the normative question is usually settled by unconscious consensus, the salient question at the beginning of federalisms is typically the technical one.) But even if the original question of adopting federalism is purely technical, still, once federalism has been established and once a federalism has reached that degree of centralization previously described as category B, the question of whether or not it ought to be maintained is open. Presumably a society with a federal government in category B has attained sufficient unity that it is no longer necessary to use the federal device to keep the expanded society viable. So at that point a normative judgment can be made about whether or not to keep the institutions that originally permitted the expansion.

Of course, the question of whether or not federalism is worth keeping seldom arises as a matter of complete constitutional revision (*e.g.*, in Austria and Germany after each of the world wars). More frequently, the question arises in a partial form; *i.e.* "What attitude ought one to adopt on this measure that will tend to reinforce (or break down) the guarantees of federalism?" In mature and stable federalisms such as the United States or Australia, where complete constitutional revision seems unlikely in the foreseeable future, there is nevertheless a frequent opportunity to decide constitutional questions on the basis of an attitude toward federalism and this is where the partial form of the question arises.[1] Whether the question arises in its partial form or in a

[1] For a concrete example of such an occasion, consider the creation (in 1935) of the unemployment insurance system as an adjunct to the social security system. President Roosevelt, apparently out of a concern for federalism, personally decided to assign the unemployment insurance and employment service to the states, at least so his advisor Tugwell tells us. (Rexford Tugwell, "The Experimental Roosevelt," *The Political Quarterly*, Vol. 21 (1950) pp. 239-62, at p. 241.) In turning down the advice of experts, Roosevelt personally preserved, at least in a small way, the constitutional

proposal for full-scale constitutional revision is, however, irrelevant to the considerations involved in the answer. Hence, the evaluation of whether or not federalism is worth keeping need not be restrained by the infrequency of constitutional conventions. Rather it is a question that politicians in a mature federalism, especially politicians in a category B federalism, must think about almost every day.

The considerations that commonly enter into decisions on these questions are the arguments advanced in favor of maintaining (or abrogating) the guarantees to constituent units. In the following sections, we shall therefore examine these arguments and some of the evidence adduced in support of them.

I FEDERALISM AND FREEDOM — THE THEORETICAL ARGUMENT FOR RETENTION

Probably the commonest argument in public debate for support of the guarantees to constituent units is the assertion that federalism is a guarantee of freedom, followed by the prescription that, in order to preserve freedom, one must preserve federalism. Assuming, as most of us would, that freedom (whatever it is) is worth preserving, the prescription nevertheless depends on a purportedly descriptive assertion, which may or may not be true. In what way is federalism related to freedom?

The political traditions of most federally governed societies predispose most of their citizens to believe that their constitutional form (*i.e.*, federalism) encourages a state of affairs (*i.e.*, freedom) that is almost universally approved. And in the traditions of both Anglo-American and Latin-American federalisms this predisposition has been reinforced by the identification of

---

guarantees of federalism. Whether or not he was wise to do so is, of course, another matter. Since the federal part of this system has been quietly and effectively administered, whereas the state part has been the center of much political turbulence and has often been charged with inefficiency, the experts were probably right from an administrative point of view. But constitutional considerations may be more important than administrative ones. What concerns us here, however, is not the correctness or incorrectness of Roosevelt's action, but simply the opportunity he had to decide a policy question on the basis of an interpretation of federalism.

the spirit of federalism with the notion of local self-government, which in turn is often identified with freedom.

But despite these predispositions of the tradition, there are also some *a priori* reasons to be sceptical about the truth of the assertion that federalism encourages freedom. There are, for example, a number of societies that keep a high degree of freedom without the use of federalism and, on the other hand, a number of federalisms simultaneously have been dictatorships. Local self-government and personal freedom both coexist with a highly centralized unitary government in Great Britain and the Vargas dictatorship in Brazil managed to coexist with federalism.

In the United States, moreover, we have even more reasons to be sceptical about the truth of the assertion when we observe that the most persistent exponents of "states' rights" — a doctrine that makes much of the freedom-encouraging features of federalism — have been those who use the doctrine as a veiled defense first of slavery, then of civil tyranny. Here it seems that federalism may have more to do with destroying freedom than with encouraging it.

Clearly the relationship, if any, between federalism and freedom is not immediately clear and deserves further investigation.

The traditional argument, which derives from *The Federalist* papers and which has been reiterated continually by advocates of states' rights in all federal systems, is the assertion that concentrated power is dangerous, a position best expressed in Acton's aphorism that power tends to corrupt and absolute power corrupts absolutely. Federalism is said to be a device to prevent absolute power and therefore to prevent tyranny. I do not think we need to take this argument very seriously. It is based on a wise saw that has the same standing in the study of politics that weather wisdom has in the study of meteorology. The aphorism is not true — indeed, sometimes its opposite is.[2] And indeed, even if it were true, there is no assurance that separating power is the appropriate way to prevent tyranny. The separation may actually promote tyranny by its constant frustration of majorities which,

[2] See Arnold Rogow and Harold Lasswell, *Power, Corruption and Rectitude* (New York: Prentice-Hall, 1963).

in their frustration, come to behave tyrannically.[3] So let us leave aside the traditional argument, which is at best folk wisdom, and examine the relationship between federalism and freedom *de novo*.

Of course, though we know fairly well what "federalism" means, we have at best a confused notion of what "freedom" means. So before we can go further, the word "freedom" must be defined. And many volumes have been written on this subject without conspicuous success in reaching agreement. Owing to the tradition of controversy over the meaning of this word, we do know, however, that one of the variables involved in the notion is the specific reference to persons. That is, one elementary question about freedom is: "freedom for whom?"

The question arises in this way: Given a society with a multiplicity of goals (and surely all societies with federal governments satisfy this assumption) and given the possibility that the achievement of goal A renders the achievement of another goal, B, unlikely or impossible. Then, when one speaks of freedom, one must specify whether one means freedom for the supporters of goal A or for those of goal B. If political life were conveniently arranged so that all feasible goals were compatible with one another, then this question could not arise. But usually we do not find such neat dovetailing of aspirations. And so in the presence of conflicting goals, a definition of freedom must always specify freedom for whom.

One convenient answer that some theories of freedom have offered is "the majority," which is unfortunately a highly artificial creation of rules of voting. Owing to this artificiality, therefore, other theories of freedom have suggested that freedom involves liberty for minorities to achieve their goals. The first kind of answer solves the problem in a somewhat arbitrary fashion, whereas the second kind begs the question completely.

But since this book has no space to pursue the problem of the meaning of freedom, we shall merely assume the existence of two kinds, majoritarian and minoritarian, and then inquire whether or

[3] See William H. Riker, *Democracy in the United States* (New York: Macmillan, 1953) Chapter 4.

not it is theoretically true that federalism is a guarantee of either kind.

Considering, first, majoritarian freedom, it seems fairly obvious that federalism cannot at all be a guarantee of this kind of freedom; but rather can actually be an impediment. The effect of allowing ultimate decision at two different levels of government (which is the essence of the federal relationship) is that the losers at the national level may reverse the decision at the constituent level. Thus, the losers nationally may become the winners locally, which of course negates the national decision in at least portions of the federal nation. Thereby, of course, the freedom of the national majority is infringed upon by local majorities.

A notorious example of such negation is the reversal of decision on civil rights for Negroes in the Southern and border states. The original national decision, taken by a narrow majority in the Civil War era, was soon reversed by local decisions in the South and along the border — where, of course, most Negroes lived. As a consequence, the Civil War decisions were thoroughly negated for most Negroes until sufficient numbers migrated northward and reawakened interest in again enforcing the old and, in recent years, frequently reaffirmed national decision.

To one who believes in the majoritarian notion of freedom, it is impossible to interpret federalism as other than a device for minority tyranny. At the present time in the United States (*i.e.*, from roughly 1954 to that future time, if it ever comes, when most Negroes have full citizen rights) the chief question of public morals is whether or not the national decision will be enforced. To those who wish to enforce it, the plea for states' rights or for maintaining the guarantees of federalism is simply a hypocritical plea for the special privilege to disregard the national majority and, of course, to permit one minority, segregationist Southern whites, to tyrannize over another minority, the Southern Negroes. When freedom is defined as the right of self-direction for majorities, then the assertion that federalism promotes freedom is simply a hypocritical falsehood.

Considering, in the second place, minoritarian freedom, which is usually presented as the freedom of a minority to preserve its civil rights against a tyrannical majority, it is apparent, I shall argue, that for this kind of freedom federalism is, if not an impediment, still quite irrelevant.

Minoritarian freedom can be interpreted either as (1) the right of minorities to have a chance to become majorities and thus to make policy or (2) the right of minorities to make policy without becoming majorities. The first interpretation; *i.e.*, the right to the chance to make policy, is in practice the maintenance of civil liberties so that prospective majorities will not be destroyed before they become such. The latter interpretation, though often set forth as the abstract ideal of freedom, is of course simply a rationale of confusion. Given, as previously, the existence of conflicting social goals, then the guarantee of the right of minorities to make policy merely assures the simultaneous existence of contradictory policies.

If minoritarian freedom is the right to have a chance to make policy, then federalism is undoubtedly an impediment to freedom in many circumstances and irrelevant to it in others. Federalism is a guarantee to constituent units of the *right* to make policy, not of the *chance* to make policy. Thus it grants far more than is necessary for freedom. The analysis works out as follows: Suppose the constituent unit granted the right to make policy agrees for the most part with the kind of policy that would be made by the national officials. Then the right to make policy means relatively little and in general federalism is irrelevant to the maintenance of freedom. Suppose, however, that the constituent unit does not so agree; then the right to make policy allows it to impinge on the right of local minorities to become majorities. This is exactly what has happened in the American South where, under its freedom to make policy, the local majority (which is a minority nationally) has deprived the local minority of its civil rights (even though that local minority has close links with the national majority). In short, federalism that grants *more* local autonomy than is necessary for freedom and civil liberty encourages local tyranny, even when freedom is narrowly interpreted as the grant of the right to minorities to have a chance to become majorities.

If, on the other hand, minoritarian freedom is the right to make policy; *i.e.*, to allow minorities to create confusion, then federalism is again irrelevant to freedom in some circumstances and a positive hindrance to freedom in others. One may distinguish the circumstances according to whether or not it costs the society more to obtain uniformity than uniformity is worth. Consider an instance in which the cost of uniformity is greater than the reward: women's clothing. At numerous times in many societies sumptuary laws and laws against nudity have been passed and frequently they have been enforced only briefly. Presumably in such instances of laxity the cost of enforcement against numerous minorities of one is greater than the reward of uniformity. When enforcement costs more than the reward, federalism is irrelevant to freedom. If freedom is the grant to minorities of one of the right to decide, *e.g.*, on physical decoration, then the right of constituent units to make policy they probably will not care to enforce against minorities is a meaningless grant. In such an instance, federalism has nothing to do with freedom, although it may guarantee tyranny.

But when national uniformity is worth more than confusion, then federalism is an impediment to freedom because it deprives the national majority of the chance to eliminate the excess costs of confusion. Consider, for example, the matter of civil rights for Negroes in the United States. The grant to constituent units to make policy on this question has meant at least the following consequences: For the last century approximately 10 per cent of the people have been denied civil rights. Those so denied have been a kind of *lumpenproletariat* and hence a drain on the whole society. In short, the grant of autonomy to local majorities to create confused policies has resulted in a cost to the whole society that is probably greater than the cost of uniformity. At least, so the present restiveness of the national majority toward Southern whites' practices of tyranny so indicates. In such an instance, we may infer that, when the costs of the consequences of federalism are greater than the costs of enforcing uniformity, local tyrannies are also national tyrannies because they prevent national majorities from reducing costs. For example, the national costs of putting up with the consequences of Southern bigotry are so great that the permission to enforce bigotry locally constitutes a cost on the whole nation, a cost which is presumably greater than the cost of enforcing desegregation. In this instance, therefore, federalism is an impediment to the freedom of everybody except segregationist whites in the South.

In summary, the abstract assertion that federalism is a guarantee of freedom is undoubtedly false. If this assertion is intended as a description of nature, then it is manifestly false, as shown by counterinstances of the coexistence of federalism and dictatorship. If it is, however, intended as a theoretical assertion about an abstract relationship undisturbed by other institutional arrangements, then it is still false. If freedom is interpreted in a majoritarian way, then the assertion is invariably false, for federalism is an impediment to freedom. If freedom is interpreted in a minoritarian way, then either federalism has nothing to do with freedom or federalism is again an impediment to freedom.

II THE HIGH COST OF UNIFORMITY — THE PRACTICAL ARGUMENT FOR RETENTION

The most frequently presented practical argument for the maintenance of the federal guarantees to the constituent units is that the cost of national decision making is greater than the reward that might be obtained from it. This argument is usually presented as a defense of expediency (*e.g.*, that it would cost more in prospective civil disturbance to integrate the schools of Mississippi than can presently be gained from this action). But sometimes it is also presented as a moral good (*e.g.*, that a positive value is obtained from diversity of culture). (The latter was a favorite argument of Justice Holmes, who interpreted the states as laboratories for solving public problems.) In either form, however, this argument is essentially an economic one involving a kind of cost analysis of constitutional forms.[4]

[4] An earlier attempt to apply a quasi-economic analysis to the costs of federalism is: J. Roland Pennock, "Federal and Unitary Government — Disharmony and Frustration," *Behavioral Science*, Vol. 4 (1959) pp. 147-57. This article contains an *ad hoc* and tendentious model from which calculations are made of the "harmony (or lessened frustration) which it is the peculiar genius of federalism to achieve." By conveniently ignoring what are here called external costs, *e.g.*, those imposed on the majority when the minority is permitted to make rules, the author finds that federalism lessens the frustrations of a minority, which, of course, no one has ever denied. The unanswered question is: At whose expense is the frustration relieved?

National decision making is in the abstract more efficient than local decision making on every issue. That is, assuming uniformity is itself costless, it is cheaper on any subject of legislation to have a uniform rule, which is made by a majority, than not to have uniformity. There are at least two strong theoretical reasons for this circumstance. For one thing there is some saving in uniformity; and for another, there is less likelihood of a minority imposing high external costs on the majority. Considering the first and lesser reason, it is apparent that there is some saving in personal learning to have something like nationally uniform rules of the road. If a red light meant different things in different localities it is highly likely that the cost of enforcement of road rules would increase enormously. But the more important saving through uniformity is the minimization of the external costs imposed on individuals when minorities are allowed to legislate a minority policy. These costs are, of course, very high when two minority policies are in direct conflict. But even when they do not seem to be in direct conflict, external costs may still be inordinately high. Consider the sum of the costs to individuals when there are different minimum wages in different localities. There is then much likelihood of capital flow from the high-wage localities to the low-wage localities for all those industries in which labor represents a high proportion of the cost. Aside from the imposition of a nationally uniform minimum wage, the only way that high-wage localities may counter this capital flow is by reducing the minimum wage level. Thus the localities with the low minimum wage are permitted to set this wage nationally. For all the localities that would like to have the high wage, the imposition of the low wage is, of course, a high external cost. Since only the lowest-wage locality will be satisfied, all other localities will suffer these external costs. The obvious way to reduce this cost is to impose a national policy. It is this possibility that accounts for the greater efficiency of uniform rules. The only circumstances in which the uniform policy would not reduce external costs over local policies would be when the low-wage locality constituted a national majority. But in this case, the supposedly local policy is in fact imposed by a national majority and is thus a uniform policy. Hence in all cases a uniform policy is cheaper from the point of view of external costs than a non-uniform policy.

Or consider the savings from uniformity in the regulation of morality rather than the regulation of the economy. Given the possibility of variation in divorce codes among constituent units, divorce may be easier to obtain in one jurisdiction than in another. Then, so long as some provision like the full faith and credit clause of the United States Constitution exists—and all federalisms have something like it—it follows that the code that will in fact regulate is the one with easiest divorce. We have an excellent example of this in the United States, where the national scandal of excessively large numbers of divorces and the concomitant scandal of ill-considered marriages are both the consequences of a variation in divorce codes. The existence of a few jurisdictions that grant divorces on the most trivial grounds and after only the briefest periods of residence are sufficient to render nugatory the more restrictive grounds and longer residence requirements of most other states. Thus the different moral standards of a few states, the codes of which seem to have been motivated more by a concern for tourist business than by any convictions one way or another about family stability, have the effect of imposing easy divorce on all jurisdictions. The external costs of the existence of what most citizens of most states regard as low moral standards are thus very high for the probably overwhelming majority that opposes easy divorce. Uniformity of divorce laws could materially lighten these costs for the majority, although it might raise costs for Nevada lawyers.

It seems clear on the basis of both theory and example that uniform national decision making is invariably more efficient, *i.e.*, less costly in undesired impositions on other people, than is local decision making. This is simply to say that decisions made by a majority hurt fewer people than do decisions made by minorities. Since constituent governments are invariably minorities in the nation, the maintenance of federal guarantees to constituent units assures that the whole society must bear some extra and unnecessary external costs.

So far, however, we have considered the cost of decision making only in a vacuum. Even if national decision making is clearly more efficient in decreasing external costs, it still may be more expensive than local decision making because of (1) costs of decision making and (2) costs of enforcement.

Costs of decision making are those incurred in the process of assembling a coalition of the size necessary to make a decision. As the requirements increase from minorities (*e.g.*, majorities in a constituent unit) to majorities (*i.e.*, a national majority), the cost of making side-payments to reluctant members (*i.e.*, logrolling) and of negotiating with all prospective members increases greatly. The cost of national decision making may well be greater than the rewards obtained from eliminating anarchy. Consider, for example, standards of beach clothing for females. Possibly a majority of people in the United States are offended by the appearance of bikinis and, were the decision costless, they would be glad to prohibit them. But, in fact, the decision is not costless: Some effort must be expended on defining what is offensive and what is not; more effort must be expended on finding the people who make up this majority; and finally additional effort must be expended on bringing them together in a group for action. In this imaginary example, the cost of decision is clearly very high, whereas the sum of the rewards to the majority is probably relatively low. Quite possibly the decision costs exceed the rewards.

Costs of enforcement are those incurred in the process of enforcing a majority decision against a recalcitrant minority. These costs vary with (1) the relative size of the minority, (2) the intensity of feeling of the minority, and (3) the ability of the minority to resist enforcement. It makes a difference for the existence of a national policy of prohibition, for example, whether or not most of the people are convinced teetotalers. In the United States during the prohibition era, the minority of regular users of alcohol was almost as large as the group of teetotalers, if indeed not larger. Hence enforcement was exceptionally costly. In India, on the other hand, where a much larger proportion of the population consists of teetotalers and where the indigenous pharmacopoeia includes a variety of drugs with physiological and social effects similar to those of alcohol, the enforcement of prohibition is relatively less costly. Again it makes a difference for the existence of a national policy of assessing an income tax whether or not the prosperous and the rich believe deeply that they should not be taxed. Thus, in the United States, the prosperous and the rich accept the basic notion of the tax and hence usually obey the exact letter of the law. The existence of this attitude means that enforcement officers are freed to pursue the minority of dishonest taxpayers. Hence the income tax works pretty well as the basic tax of the nation. In India, on the other hand, the justice of the tax is not as widely acknowledged by the prosperous and rich. Hence enforcement agents must spend most of their efforts on what would elsewhere be regarded as ordinary collection. As a consequence, enforcement is costly and the income tax cannot be used as the basic tax system. Finally, it makes a difference for the existence of a national policy of civil rights for depressed classes whether or not those who oppress them can successfully defend the oppression both practically and philosophically. Again compare India and the United States, in both of which national decisions have repeatedly condemned the oppression of in one case the Scheduled Castes and in the other case Negroes. In both cases there are good practical devices to avoid enforcement; *e.g.*, the relative unanimity of the rural upper classes on the desirability of resistance. In both cases there are also good philosophical grounds to resist enforcement; *e.g.*, the doctrine of states' rights in the United States and the doctrines of Hinduism in India. But the outlook for enforcement of the national policy is much better in the United States than in India simply because (1) the unanimity of the rural upper classes is nationwide in India whereas in the United States it is breaking down and indeed is limited to two or three very recalcitrant states and (2) the doctrine of states' rights is increasingly regarded as a sham for oppression whereas, owing to the new nationalism, the doctrines of Hinduism are held to even more tenaciously than before. Negroes are likely to obtain civil rights sooner than untouchables simply because the ability of their oppressors to resist enforcement is less.

In this analysis of the costs of national decision making in relation to decision making by constituent units, we have thus identified three kinds of charges:

(1) the profits of uniformity, symbolized by "*U*", which are invariably positive in sign because majority decision is always better than anarchy;
(2) the costs of making decisions, symbolized by "*D*", which are invariably negative in sign because it is more costly to assemble a majority than a minority; and
(3) the costs of enforcement of decisions, symbolized by "*E*", which are also invariably negative in sign because the existence of a majority implies the existence of a minority that must be coerced.

The practical argument in favor of maintaining the federal guarantees to the constituent units is that $U + D + E \leqslant 0$. Of course, this argument cannot be uttered generally for it would mean the desirability of the dissolution of the federalism. Rather, it must be uttered in particular instances and where it is asserted after a rough assessment of the values of *U*, *D*, and *E*. Since the argument cannot be asserted generally except as a proposal for civil war, one wonders about what kind of instances it seems reasonable in. In short, what kinds of circumstances minimize the sum of *U*, *D*, and *E*?

It is impossible, of course, to offer an exhaustive list; but one can specify some typical circumstances. As for minimizing *U*, which of course increases the likelihood that the inequation $U + D + E \leqslant 0$ will hold, the most important circumstance probably is that the policy field will be fairly low on the preference schedules of most of the members of the prospective majority. If most people don't care much whether or not policy in a specific area (*e.g.*, women's beachwear) is anarchic, then the positive value of *U* will be low. The issue of whether or not to maintain the federal guarantee to constituent units does not, however, arise when *U* is low, for to say *U* is low is to say it concerns something to which most people are close to indifferent. So the problem is: In what circumstances, when *U* is high, is $-(D + E)$ higher?

What minimizes *D* is the existence of numerous territorial minorities, each of whose schedules of preference is quite different from others. The fact that these minorities are territorially based gives them some strength to insist on obtaining their preferences and the fact that their preference schedules are different renders the bargaining process expensive. India is a federalism in which, *a priori*, one might expect D to be very low in many areas of public policy.

What minimizes E is the intensity of feeling of a minority, a defensive sense that their separateness is both under attack and worth preserving. Coupled with this sense of separateness must also be a large territorial and population base so that the minority actually has some strength to resist enforcement. Canada is a federalism in which, *a priori*, one might expect E to be very low in many areas of public policy.

The practical argument for the maintenance of the federal guarantees to the constituent units, *viz.*, that $U + D + E \leqslant 0$, is clearly dependent upon the calculations of politicians and citizens about the magnitudes of U, D, and E in particular sets of circumstances. In general, if there are numerous areas *of importance* in which it is agreed that the inequation $U + D + E \leqslant 0$ holds, then the argument in favor of maintaining the guarantees is good. If not, then the argument fails. For me, the argument is reasonable and impressive with respect to such federalisms as Canada and India, but it is specious and unreasonable with respect to such federalisms as the United States, Germany, Austria, and Australia.

III ABROGATING THE GUARANTEES

The main theoretical argument in favor of abrogating the federal guarantees to constituent units has already been developed in connection with arguments for maintaining them: Decisions made by constituent units are invariably minority decisions that impose high external costs on the national majority. This assertion is wholly irrefutable on the level of theory, although it may be shown, as I have also indicated, that in particular instances it may cost more to remove the external costs than is saved with uniformity. But even though the assertion is theoretically irrefutable some effort has been expended in showing that it is not necessarily true in all circumstances. Cohen and Grodzins, for example, have attempted to show that state fiscal policies in the United States do not always conflict with national policies.[5] And they did indeed show that the state policies are less sharply in conflict with national policy than had previously been believed.[6] But to show that the anarchy of numerous minority decisions does not impose external costs as high as Hansen and Perloff believed is also to admit that external costs do exist. Indeed, the chief significance of Cohen and Grodzins' work is that they found a way to measure them. The existence of external costs is an invitation to eliminate them, which is the chief theoretical argument in favor of abrogating the guarantees.

Unfortunately the theoretical arguments, though theoretically decisive, are practically uncertain because of the uncertainty surrounding the magnitudes of U, D, and E. Hence, to decide in particular instances whether or not to abrogate the guarantees it is necessary to examine the cultural and institutional setting of the constitution. The appropriate questions are: Who benefits by the imposition of external costs on others? or, What minority is allowed by the federal device to impose its rules on the majority? According as one disapproves or approves of the values and purposes of these minorities, one favors or opposes the abrogation of the guarantees. One does not decide on the merits of federalism by an examination of federalism in the abstract, but rather on its actual meaning for particular societies.

What minorities benefit from the grant to make policy in:

The United States? The main beneficiary throughout American history has been the Southern whites, who have been given the freedom to oppress Negroes, first as slaves and later as a depressed caste. Other minorities have from time to time also managed to obtain some of these benefits; *e.g.*, special business interests have been allowed to regulate themselves, especially in the

[5] Jacob Cohen and Morton Grodzins, "How Much Economic Sharing in American Federalism," *American Political Science Review*, Vol. 57 (1963) pp. 5-23.

[6] Alvin Hansen and Harvey Perloff, *State and Local Finance in the National Economy* (New York: Norton, 1944).

era from about 1890 to 1936, by means of the judicial doctrine of dual federalism, which eliminated both state and national regulation of such matters as wage rates and hours of labor. But the significance of federal benefits to economic interests pales beside the significance of benefits to the Southern segregationist whites. The judgment to be passed on federalism in the United States is therefore a judgment on the values of segregation and racial oppression.

Canada? The main beneficiary in Canada from the beginning has been the French-speaking minority, whose dissidence was the original occasion for adopting federalism and is the justification for retaining it today. Secondarily, as in the United States, commercial interests have also benefited by escaping regulation. But since the French Canadians have no particular alliance with business, economic conservatives have benefited less in Canada than in the United States (where Southern segregationists have a tacit alliance with economic conservatives). That is, the French speakers have seen less reason to rig the competitive market to the advantage of owners (as against workers or consumers) because very few French Canadians have been owners.

Brazil? The most significant minority benefiting from Brazilian federalism is the class of large landowners, especially in the relatively underdeveloped north and east. Although Brazilian federalism lacks the tone of racism associated with federalism in the United States, the social consequences are the same: the maintenance of a class of poor and inefficient farm laborers for the presumed benefit of agrarian landlords.

India? Indian federalism is probably too youthful to identify the main beneficiaries of the privilege of minority decision making. But two kinds of minorities have tended to emphasize states' rights: non-Hindi-speaking groups (who, together, are of course a majority) and landlords in the least-developed agricultural areas.

Australia? Since no single minority has been able to exploit the advantages of minority decision exclusively or for long periods of time, it is difficult to identify the main beneficiary. Nevertheless, it seems that commercial interests have been granted freedom from regulation more than any other group.

Germany? Originally, federalism was intended to grant the right of minority decision to the non-Prussian southwest. But the significance of this minority has declined in the successive transformations of German federalism so that today it is difficult to specify who, if anyone, benefits most.

The foregoing survey of several federal systems suggests the wide variety of kinds of minorities that may benefit especially from the privilege to legislate. The kind of minorities that appears most frequently on this list is business and agricultural owners. It is not difficult to understand why. In capitalistic nations conflicting economic interests are engaged constantly in an effort to rig the competitive system in their favor. Those groups which constitute national majorities, *e.g.*, workers, farm laborers, consumers, etc. are those which might be expected to benefit most from majoritarian decision processes. To allow minoritarian processes is, therefore, to deprive the very large groups of their chance to influence outcomes. Of course, the minority most likely to benefit from the chance to manipulate the market is that of the owners, business or agricultural according to whether the nation is primarily industrial or agrarian.

But it is not always or only the owners who benefit, for, as the brief survey indicates, linguistic or racist minorities may also thrive on federalism. One possible classification of federalism, especially appropriate for passing judgment on the desirability of retaining federalism, is by the main beneficiaries of the chance of minorities to legislate for the whole. A moral judgment must be passed in each instance and for comparative purposes I submit a list (Table 6.1) of the main characteristics of the main federalisms. It is notable that the federalism of the United States is unique in fostering racism.

IV IS FEDERALISM WORTH KEEPING?

One seldom has the opportunity to rewrite whole constitutions so the question of keeping or abandoning federalism can seldom arise. But a related question does frequently arise: What ought to be one's posture toward federalism? Should one always attempt to maintain or abrogate the guarantees to the constituent units?

In pure theory, the answer is that what one ought to seek to abrogate for federalism is a system of minority decision that imposes high external costs on everybody other than the minority. But practically the answer is not so clear, for the costs of decision and enforcement may outweigh the advantages of majoritarianism when the minority favored by federalism is passionate in its convictions.

Table 6.1 MAIN BENEFICIARIES OF FEDERALISM

	Capitalists	*Landlords*	*Linguistic minorities*	*Racists*
United States	X	X		X
Canada	X		X	
Mexico		X		
Brazil	X	X		
Argentina	X	X		
Australia	X			
India		X	X	
Switzerland	X		X	
Germany	X			
Yugoslavia			X	
Soviet Union			X	

Since the actual calculation of rewards and costs from abrogating federal guarantees is simply a rough "more or less" necessarily calculated by interested parties, one probably cannot even use a cost analysis in judging actual federalisms. Rather one must look to what they do and determine what minorities they favor. If one approves the goals and values of the privileged minority, one should approve the federalism. Thus, if in the United States one approves of Southern white racists, then one should approve of American federalism. If, on the other hand, one disapproves of the values of the privileged minority, one should disapprove of federalism. Thus, if in the United States one disapproves of racism, one should disapprove of federalism.

Suggestions for further reading

I COMPARATIVE WORKS

General works on federalism are few in number and spotty in quality. The survey that has dominated the study of this subject for many years is K. C. Wheare, *Federal Government* (London: Oxford University Press, 1946, 3rd ed., 1953). It is highly legalistic in tone and displays very little understanding of political realities. A far better work, even though it is a volume of disconnected essays, is: A. W. MacMahon, ed., *Federalism: Mature and Emergent* (New York: Columbia University Press, 1955). Several of the essays in this volume, especially those by David Truman and Edward Weidner, are notable for transcending both the legalistic and the normative categories in which federalism is usually discussed. A straightforwardly legalistic analysis, with little pretense and much perception, is Edward McWhinney, *Comparative Federalism* (Toronto: University of Toronto Press, 1962). A none-too-successful attempt to break out of the legalistic mold is S. P. Aiyar, *Federalism and Social Change* (New York: Asia Publishing House, 1961). Finally, mention should be made of Robert R. Bowie and Carl J. Friedrich, eds., *Studies in Federalism* (Boston: Little, Brown and Company, 1954), which is useful because of the vast amount of constitutional detail summarized in it. Students should be warned, however, that though it purports to be simply a collation, it unconsciously offers an interpretation of federalism that is, because unconscious, both conventional and unsophisticated.

Several comparative studies of special features of federalism ought also to be mentioned: William Livingston, *Federalism and Constitutional Change* (Oxford: Oxford University Press, 1956) is, by reason of its subject matter, highly legalistic, but nevertheless it is an illuminating analysis of this feature of federalism. A. H. Birch, *Federalism, Finance, and Social Legislation in Canada, Australia and the United States* (London: Oxford University Press, 1955) displays about as comprehensive an appreciation of the realities of federalism as any volume in this bibliography. Finally, W. K. Hicks, F. G. Carnell, J. R. Hicks, W. T. Newlyn, and A. H. Birch, *Federalism and Economic Growth in Underdeveloped Countries* (London: George Allen and Unwin, 1961) contains several papers, especially the one by Carnell, with a broad understanding of federalism.

II STUDIES OF PARTICULAR FEDERAL SYSTEMS

Under this rubric, I distinguish two categories of books according to the main questions of this study: (a) those concerned with the occasion for adopting federalism and (b) those concerned with the maintenance and operation of federalism. In listing suggested readings by countries I shall attempt to distinguish between the works most useful for (a) and those most useful for (b). Naturally, this list does not purport to be exhaustive, for indeed I have space to mention only the most important works for each country.

United States. (a) A good history of the convention at which centralized federalism was invented is Carl Van Doren, *The Great Rehearsal* (New York: Viking Press, 1948). The student who wishes to follow for himself the drama of that invention can consult: Max Farrand, *Records of the Federal Convention of 1787* (New Haven: Yale University Press, 4 vols., 1911 and 1938) or, in an excellent abbreviation, Winton V. Stolberg, *The Federal*

Convention and the Formation of the Union of the American States (New York: Liberal Arts Press, 1958). (b) Studies of particular federalistic institutions are Daniel J. Elezar, *The American Partnership* (Chicago: University of Chicago Press, 1962), William H. Riker, *Soldiers of the States* (Washington, D.C.: Public Affairs Press, 1957): and Jane Perry Clark, *The Rise of the New Federalism* (New York: Columbia University Press, 1938). A survey of the state of administrative relationships between the nation and the states is set forth in the publications of the Commission on Inter-Governmental Relations and is summarized in its *Report* (Washington, D.C.: Government Printing Office, 1955). A detailed and conscientious survey of both administrative and political relationships is set forth in W. Brooke Graves, *American Intergovernmental Relations* (New York, Charles Scribner's Sons, 1964).

Canada. (a) A good introduction to the history of confederation is found in R. M. Dawson, *The Government of Canada* (Toronto Press, 1952), pp. 1-59. (b) Although I do not like to cite relatively inaccessible material, I cannot forbear mentioning Steven Muller, *Federalism and the Party System in Canada* (mimeographed, paper presented at American Political Science Association meeting, St. Louis, 1961), for this is without question the most sensitive interpretation of Canadian federalism. The comments in Birch, *op. cit.*, are also very good on Canada. The classic governmental investigation is the *Report* of the Rowell-Sirois Commission, which is now, unfortunately, rather out of date. See also A. R. M. Lower, *et al.*, *Evolving Canadian Federalism* (Durham: Duke University Press, 1958).

Australia. Gordon Greenwood, *The Future of Australian Federalism* (Melbourne: Melbourne University Press, 1946) is excellent under both rubrics (a) and (b). Additionally for (b) one should mention J. D. B. Miller, *Australian Government and Politics* (London: Duckworth, 1954).

India. (a) The definitive work on the formation of Indian federalism is yet to be written. In the meantime, M. V. Pylee, *Constitutional Government in India* (Bombay: Asia Publishing House,

1960) is very good on constitutional detail, and V. P. Menon, *The Integration of the Indian States* (New York: Macmillan, 1956) is excellent on one phase of the politics of the federalism. (b) Nothing very illuminating has yet been written about the operation of Indian federalism, but the best that has come to my attention is Paul Appleby, *Public Administration in India* (Delhi: Manager of Publications, 1953).

Pakistan. For (a), G. W. Chaudhury, *Constitutional Development in Pakistan* (London: Longmans, 1959) is good and for (b) Muhammad Asad, *The Principles of State and Government in Islam* (Berkeley: University of California Press, 1961), is useful.

Malaysia. Nothing substantial has yet been written under either rubric about either Malaya or Malaysia.

Nigeria and Rhodesia. (a) Donald S. Rothchild, *Toward Unity in Africa* (Washington, D.C., Public Affairs Press, 1960) is a good survey of origins. The African experience with federalism has been too brief to occasion much work on its operation. See also Kalu Ezera *Constitutional Developments in Nigeria* (Cambridge: Cambridge University Press, 1960).

British West Indies. Both Morley Ayearst, *British West Indies. The Search for Self-Government* (London: George Allen & Unwin, 1960) and David Lowenthal, *The West Indies Federation* (New York: Columbia University Press, 1961) are useful.

Switzerland. On the formal constitution, see Christopher Hughes, *The Federal Constitution of Switzerland* (Oxford: Oxford University Press, 1954); on its contemporary operation, see George A. Codding, *The Federal Government of Switzerland* (Boston: Houghton Mifflin Co., 1961).

Germany. (a) The background of German federalism is well analyzed in Arnold Brecht, *Federalism and Regionalism in Germany* (New York: Oxford University Press, 1945). The Weimar federalism is discussed historically but not analytically in Erich Eyck, *A History of the Weimar Republic* (Cambridge: Harvard University Press, 1962); whereas the origin of the most recent federalism is carefully analyzed in John Ford Golay, *The Found-*

ing of the Federal Republic of Germany (Chicago: University of Chicago Press, 1958). (b) Two useful works on the operation of federalism are: Edward L. Pinney, *Federalism, Bureaucracy and Party Politics in Western Germany: The Role of the Bundesrat* (Chapel Hill: University of North Carolina Press, 1963) and Roger H. Wells, *The States in West German Federalism* (New York: Bookman Associates, 1961).

Austria. Rudolph Schlesinger, *Federalism in Central and Eastern Europe* (London: Kegan Paul, 1945) is excellent as far as it goes in time and so is Charles A. Gulick, *Austria from Hapsburg to Hitler* (Berkeley: University of California Press, 1948, 2 vols.). Unfortunately no adequate work on the most recent federalism in Austria exists.

Soviet Union. The best study of the formation of the Soviet Union is in Schlesinger, *op. cit.*

Yugoslavia. The federal features of the Yugoslavian government and Titoist expansionism have not been well studied, but about the best comments are to be found in Adam Ulam, *Titoism and the Cominform* (Cambridge: Harvard University Press, 1952) and Zbigniew Brzezinski, *The Soviet Bloc* (Cambridge: Harvard University Press, 1960).

Latin America. (a) A good survey of constitution-making in Latin America is included in William W. Pierson and Frederico G. Gil, *Governments of Latin America* (New York: McGraw-Hill, 1957). Conyers Read, ed., *The Constitution Reconsidered* (New York: Columbia University Press, 1938) contains excellent essays (by C. W. Haring, J. Lloyd Mechan, and Percy A. Martin) on the origins of federalism in Latin America generally, Mexico, and Brazil. The best study in English of the political thought of the revolutionary era is Victor Andrés Belaunde, *Bolívar and the Political Thought of the Spanish American Revolution* (Baltimore: Johns Hopkins University Press, 1938). Also useful is Thomas L. Karnes, *The Failure of Union: Central America, 1824-1960* (Chapel Hill: University of North Carolina Press, 1960). (b) Although awkward in design and execution, the only survey of the contemporary operation of Latin American federalism is William Stokes, "The Centralized Federal Republics of Latin America," Institute for Studies in Federalism, *Essays in Federalism* (Claremont, Calif.: Claremont College, 1963).

On individual Latin federalisms, see, for Brazil, Joad Pondia Calogeras, *A History of Brazil*, trans. by Percy Martin (Chapel Hill: University of North Carolina Press, 1939), and Herman G. James, *The Constitutional System of Brazil* (Washington, D.C.: Carnegie Institution of Washington, 1923); for Argentina, L. S. Rowe, *The Federal System of the Argentine Republic* (Washington, D.C.: Carnegie Institution of Washington, 1921) and for Colombia, William M. Gibson, *The Constitutions of Colombia* (Durham: Duke University Press, 1948).

On Ethiopia and the Mali Federation and Congo there is little but journalism available in published form.

On Indonesia an outstanding work is: A. Arthur Schiller, *The Formation of Federal Indonesia* (The Hague: Van Hoeve, 1955).

III EVALUATIVE WORKS

Most studies of federalism that are not frankly descriptive are aggressively polemical, but there are two collections of essays, primarily evaluative in nature without excessive concern for or against states' rights. These are: Robert A. Goldwin, ed., *A Nation of States: Essays on the American Federal System* (Chicago: Rand-McNally, 1963) which contains excellent evaluative essays by Morton Grodzins and Martin Diamond plus some polemical essays; and the American Assembly, *The Forty-Eight States* (New York: Columbia University Press, 1955) which contains excellent evaluative essays by James Fesler and Harvey Mansfield.

Index